Reading Scripture
with the Church

Reading Scripture
with the Church

Toward a Hermeneutic
for Theological Interpretation

A. K. M. Adam

Stephen E. Fowl

Kevin J. Vanhoozer

Francis Watson

Baker Academic
Grand Rapids, Michigan

© 2006 by A. K. M. Adam, Stephen E. Fowl, Kevin J. Vanhoozer, and Francis Watson

Published by Baker Academic
a division of Baker Publishing Group
P.O. Box 6287, Grand Rapids, MI 49516-6287
www.bakeracademic.com

Printed in the United States of America

Library of Congress Cataloging-in-Publication Data
Reading Scripture with the church : toward a hermeneutic for theological interpretation / A. K. M. Adam . . . [et al.].
        p.   cm.
    Includes bibliographical references and indexes.
    ISBN 10: 0-8010-3173-7 (pbk.)
    ISBN 978-0-8010-3173-1 (pbk.)
    1. Bible—Hermeneutics. 2. Bible—Criticism, interpretation, etc.
I. Adam, A. K. M. (Andrew Keith Malcolm), 1957–
BS476.R425 2006
220.601—dc22   2006013929

Contents

Contributors

A. K. M. Adam (Ph.D., Duke University) is professor of New Testament at Seabury-Western Theological Seminary. His authored or edited books include *What Is Postmodern Biblical Criticism?*, *Making Sense of New Testament Theology*, and *A Handbook of Postmodern Biblical Interpretation*.

Stephen E. Fowl (Ph.D., University of Sheffield) is professor of theology at Loyola College in Maryland. His authored or edited books include *Engaging Scripture: A Model for Theological Interpretation* and *The Theological Interpretation of Scripture: Classic and Contemporary Readings*.

Kevin J. Vanhoozer (Ph.D., University of Cambridge) is research professor of systematic theology at Trinity Evangelical Divinity School. His authored or edited books include *Dictionary of Theological Interpretation of the Bible*, *Is There a Meaning in This Text?*, and *The Bible, the Reader, and the Morality of Literary Knowledge*.

Francis Watson (D.Phil., University of Oxford) is professor of New Testament exegesis at the University of Aberdeen. His authored or edited books include *Paul and the Hermeneutics of Faith*, *Text and Truth: Redefining Biblical Theology*, and *Text, Church, and World: Biblical Interpretation in Theological Perspective*.

Preface

The history of biblical interpretation is customarily presented as a series of formal disquisitions, with professors and clergy declaiming long-winded lectures from podium or pulpit (often in Latin). This institutionalized history obviously emphasizes the eminent, public monuments of an intellectual and spiritual history. It misses, however, some of the vitally productive moments when thoughtful readers of Scripture work out their interpretations in animated dialogue with one another—around a kitchen table, over a beer at a public house, in the book display at a professional conference, in a quiet study, in a noisy living room filled with active children.

This collection's four contributors have been arguing with one another about the theological interpretation of Scripture for many years now. We have made our cases on formal academic panels and debated in the pages of technical publications, yes, but we have spent even more time hashing out our dissents and agreements in less formal, more convivial settings. These essays emerge out of an ongoing conversation of more than a decade's duration—and those discussions, in turn, arise out of a larger struggle. We share an ardent concern that the church soundly attend both to the theological weight of diverse ancient texts and to the critical investigation of those texts' grammar, milieu, and historical verisimilitude. When we trade ripostes over coffee and bagels, we argue as inheritors of a ponderous, joyous, and probably endless problem.

Of course, we represent only a small portion of the church's long-standing deliberation about Scripture and theology. Millions of souls have studied the Bible with insights that our conversation does not engage, with resources we neglect. A more expansive collection of essays would embrace contributions from women, from other cultures, from other streams of the Christian tradition, from sibling faiths, and perhaps from utterly divergent religions. Such a compendium would be stronger for the breadth of its scope. At the same time, however, a more varied roster of contributors would miss the strength that common interest and mutual trust lend to this more modest volume. These essays grow organically from the experience of hypothesis, response, review, and revision that long-standing collegial discussion makes possible.

The conversation recorded here takes place at a time during which the theological interpretation of Scripture is rising anew from a fallow interval. The aftermath of the biblical theology movement (to the extent that such a thing existed in more than a heuristic sense) yielded many fresh, powerful insights into the social settings of the biblical writers, into the ways that the individual writings hang together (or strain apart), and into the ways that the distinct scriptural texts converge and diverge. Scholars redirected some of the energy that might have gone toward exploring biblical theology toward more general hermeneutics and encountered there the uncanny torsions of postmodern thought. Readers who had long been excluded from technical study of the Bible challenged the prevalent culture's representatives to lay aside the rhetorical devices of domination. The biblical academy has begun to reckon with the difference of Scripture's significance in all the innumerable languages and dialects, with respect to racial privilege, in conjunction with the varying experiences of women and men in multifarious social environments. After so much learning and reassessment, a community of scholars has again taken up the question of the Bible's relation to theology, worship, ethics, and all the practices of everyday life.

It would be a mistake to suggest that this moment marks the inception of a new biblical theology movement. Such claims are cheap, usually mere self-congratulation and public-relations puffery. No manifesto unites the participants in the resurgent discourse of the theological interpretation of Scripture, nor do any distinctive common premises set apart a particular constituency of all so-called new biblical theologians. Still, one can point to numerous signs of an impetus to raise again, more carefully, the question of the theological interpretation of Scripture among new interlocutors. The participants to this particular colloquium—who have contributed numerous weighty volumes to the topic—are only a few of the thoughtful theologians and scholars of Scripture whose vigor and love for insight are refreshing the discipline of biblical theology. The Institute for Scriptural Reasoning, the North Park Symposium on the Theological Interpretation of Scripture (and its published proceedings in *Ex auditu*), the Scripture and Hermeneutics Seminar (with its attendant published proceedings), and the proliferation of professional groups dedicated to study of the sound, critical interpretation of the theological significance of Scripture—all testify to the vigorous efflorescence of inquiry into a topic that numerous scholars pronounced dead only a few years ago.

The four participants in these reflections on the theological interpretation of Scripture exemplify characteristics of many of their colleagues in this renewed project. Most obviously, all four accept without hesitation or defensiveness the premise that the church makes a vital contribution to their discourse. Whereas arguments over biblical theology sometimes relied exclusively on claims about impartial historical inquiry and the nature of understanding, these essayists share a sense that the church's teaching traditions complement the truth that comes to expression in the theological interpretation of Scripture. In acknowledging the pertinence of interpreters from throughout the ages, biblical theologians can draw on a richer and much more diverse range of perspectives than do their abstemiously historical colleagues. They participate in a centuries-long conversation with interpreters ancient and modern that benefits from the insights of preachers and theologians as well as secular academics.

Accordingly, these interpreters address the theological dimensions of the texts they study not as a second step after having ascertained what the text really means. The theological sense of the Bible pervades the operations by which we endeavor to arrive at meaning, as it also pervades our efforts to articulate the meaning we discern. One can certainly, quite legitimately, ponder a text's relation to antecedent texts or to contemporaneous texts—its lexicographic, syntactic, social, political, literary, and historical characteristics. In so doing, one will necessarily engage other characteristics at least superficially (or by deliberate omission). One cannot consider the political import of a text without construing the definitions and grammar by which we read the text in the first place, and when one expounds the poetic characteristics of a text without noting its liberatory (or oppressive) effects on readers' lives, one as much as claims that the political effects do not merit our attention. Thus, while one can read the Bible without reflecting on the ways that the Bible depicts God and humanity, that silence warrants the reader's inference that the theological significance of the text matters in only a secondary way—if at all. The scholars writing here refuse to trivialize the theological significance of Scripture; they recognize (and practice) the critical reading of Scripture with the conventional repertoire of textual, historical, analytical methods, but their analyses do not omit mention of, and often highlight, the ways that the Bible informs and is expounded by the church's teaching.

The four essayists in this book also share a respectful engagement with postmodern criticism. Though each takes up distinct aspects of the mercurial phenomenon of postmodern thought, none trades in the glib dismissals by which resolutely modern interpreters attempt to shore up their favored presuppositions. At the same time, none is simply "a postmodern biblical critic." Though their interpretive practices acknowledge the cogency of postmodern critique, their readings are determined less by a fascination with textual *mises-en-abîmes* or "undecidability" than by how the truth to which Scripture points comes to expression in ways that modern interpretations oversimplify (when they do not stifle them). While many biblical theologians adhere to a modern program for interpretive legitimacy and while many postmodern interpreters of the Bible show little interest in constructive theology, the authors in this book exemplify the possibility of a theological criticism informed, but not governed, by postmodern arguments.

Finally, these authors also take very seriously the importance of *action* for biblical interpretation. They refuse to isolate the practice of biblical interpretation in a closed circulation of words-about-words, insulated from the lives that adhere to (or depart from) the ways of living they see commended, or commanded, in Scripture. The theological interpretation of Scripture involves ethical concerns throughout: ethical concerns relative to interpretive method, but also ethical concerns relative to the sorts of life that prepare one to interpret Scripture truly, relative to the sorts of life that bespeak sound biblical interpretation, and especially relative to the concentrated expression of the praise of God in worship. These aspects of lived, embodied interpretation affect profoundly our academic and technical analysis of Scripture; readings cannot neglect the dimension of interpretive action without flattening their representations of God and truth, distorting by omission some of the most urgent elements of biblical exposition.

A. K. M. Adam proposes that analysts of biblical theology have gone off course to the extent that they have allowed their imaginations to be shaped by the *textuality* of Scripture. If we try to devise a biblical theology as though the Bible were an elaborate (somewhat perverse) secret message and as though our task were to write out a correct translation of that message, we will always run afoul of a misunderstanding of "meaning," how we apprehend it and how we propagate it. Instead of continuing to construe the theological interpretation of Scripture as an exercise in translating, Adam proposes that we envision biblical theology as a "signifying practice," as much a way of life as a solution to a textual conundrum.

Stephen Fowl, in turn, describes Thomas Aquinas's interpretive practice. Thomas figures prominently since he provides a durable rationale for interpreting Scripture on various levels (the fourfold hermeneutic of medieval exegesis), while he emphasizes the irreplaceably fundamental role of the literal sense of the Bible. Fowl shows, however, that Thomas does not simply rely on the spiritual senses of Scripture to account for the variety in theological interpretations; instead, Thomas ascribes multivocality to the literal sense itself. Thus, although subsequent theologians have often argued that the literal sense provides a univocal criterion that can distinguish legitimate from illegitimate interpretations, Fowl shows that Thomas's literal sense provides a bounded plurality—irreducible to a single meaning, but decisively shaped by the kind of life of discipleship that orients itself toward the Triune God to whom Christians turn in hope.

Kevin Vanhoozer returns to the performative aspect of the theological interpretation of Scripture as the touchstone of his essay. Vanhoozer explores the role of improvisational fidelity to the cues that Scripture gives us, but he keeps a careful eye on the unwavering criterion of faithful performance: God's communicative intention as definitively expressed in the Bible. The Bible constitutes a communicative action, to which its readers are called to respond by fulfilling the intention that God prepares for them there. Scripture's full meaning will not come to expression in any one of our performative interpretations—but the one true will of God, which inspired the biblical authors to write what they did, serves to authorize (or repudiate) our attempts to perpetuate the voice of Scripture in our performance.

Francis Watson fittingly concludes the series of essays by invoking the single identity of Jesus Christ, evoked in the fourfold gospel canon, as an authoritative example of the possibility and limitations of plurality. The church did not receive into its canon just any old story about Jesus. Though witnesses (oral and textual) to the ministry of Jesus told much more than the gospel canon eventually contained, Watson shows that the church fathers adhere to the canonical Gospels—and *not* others—even where they do not explicitly identify the four gospel traditions by name. The early period does not *conceal* a burgeoning abundance of equally credible alternative gospels; contrariwise, it openly manifests a confident reliance on the traditions of the four familiar Gospels that were eventually recognized by the church's canon.

The panorama of interpretive practice depicted in these essays (and the four responses) includes scenes from the early church's deliberation over how to adjudicate the gospel canon, the medieval church's discernment of levels of meaning in the biblical text, the modern church's interpretive conventions, and the postmodern church's articulation of its faith in improvisational testimony to the gospel. They involve graphical, musical, and dramaturgical interpretations of the Bible. They break open the closed cycle of "words about words about words" to evaluate the ways that interpretive practices from different realms enrich theological interpretation of Scripture. These varied frames of reference not only provide cues for fresh approaches to biblical theology, but also (and arguably more importantly) demonstrate the ways that criteria from these discourses can direct and assess the soundness of our interpretations.

We offer these essays, then, as a culmination of conversations past and a starting point for further discussion. With gratitude to the families who have indulged our proclivity to carry our vocational interests into all settings, to the colleagues who have encouraged and challenged us, to Seabury-Western Theological Seminary for hosting the Winslow Lectures that developed into these essays, we hope that these essays will introduce readers to the practice of theological interpretation with a fresh sense of the possibility, vitality, and urgent importance of this endeavor.

PART 1

ESSAYS

1

Poaching on Zion

Biblical Theology as Signifying Practice

A. K. M. ADAM

From its beginnings, the discourse concerning biblical theology has been marked by a sense of loss, of lack. Sometimes the lack was deliberate, as when biblical theologians deliberately excluded dogmatic considerations from their interpretations of biblical texts; at other times, however, they bemoaned the lack of richness, strength, and vigor that theologians and their readers sought when they turned to biblical theology. Some scholars make that lament their explicit theme; others pursue their deliberations in the silent shadow of the wound of biblical theology, aiming to revive, to mend, what has been missed.

The problems that beset biblical theology are many faceted, and only a fool would attempt to resolve all aspects of them at once. One element of these problems, however, derives from the linguistic captivity of biblical interpretation, the constricted understanding of semiotics that takes "language" as its paradigm. This narrow approach to theological meaning restricts interpretation to a model that lends itself to polemics and exclusion, to the *enclosure* of a realm of expression in which meaning's abundance can be confined to authorized, legitimized expressions. The reflections that follow will propose a hermeneutic that opens the Scriptures to interpretations that are not authorized in advance—in the trust that a biblical theology that develops out of the divine abundance of semiosis[1] will more powerfully equip the imagination of the saints for their work of ministry, for the signifying practice of making known the good news of God's joy and peace to all people.

The Background of Lack

The "lack" to which I refer comes to light in a variety of ways. The most explicit manifestation of lack comes from the titles of prominent works in the history of the field; we may take *The Strange Silence of the Bible in the Church* and *Biblical Theology in Crisis* as two examples of the genre,[2] but very little effort would disclose numerous other, more recent examples of books and essays that bemoan the absence of some elusive, desired characteristic.[3]

We should not be surprised if something seems amiss in the field of the theological interpretation of the Bible; the discourses

1. For this essay, I use "semiosis" and related terms to designate "meaning-making" in general, without specific allusion to the accounts of semiotics, semiology, seminalysis, and so on that semioticians provide in such great quantity and detail.

2. James D. Smart, *The Strange Silence of the Bible in the Church* (Philadelphia: Westminster, 1962); and Brevard S. Childs, *Biblical Theology in Crisis* (Philadelphia: Westminster, 1970).

3. Jean Daniélou diagnoses the modern lack by contrasting modern scholarship to patristic interpretations: "Few things are more disconcerting for the modern man than the Scriptural commentaries of the Fathers of the Church. On the one hand there is a fullness, both theological and spiritual, which gives to them a richness unequalled elsewhere. But at the same time modern man feels a stranger to their outlook and they cut clean through his modes of thought. Hence the depreciation, so common, of Patristic exegesis"; *Shadows to Reality: Studies in the Biblical Typology of the Fathers* (trans. Dom Wulfstan Hibberd; London: Burns & Oates, 1960), vii.

of biblical theology emerge under vexatious circumstances. If we agree to the common judgment that Johannes Gabler founded this study as an academic endeavor (in his own inaugural lecture of 1787) then we can detect several ominous midwives attending the discipline's birth. Gabler proposes in the lecture's title ("On the Proper Distinction between Biblical and Dogmatic Theology") that biblical theology serve as a limit and guide to systematic theology. The very opening words of Gabler's essay invoke "the fatal discords of the various sects."[4] In the course of his essay, he contrasts biblical theology with the simple faith of pious people—biblical theology must be more learned, more rigorous than simple religion.[5] He distinguishes biblical theology from spiritual interpretation: "Let us not by applying tropes forge new dogmas about which the authors themselves never thought."[6] Gabler advocates a synthetic, critical approach in preference to what he took to be literalism and proof-texting.

Over the two centuries since Gabler gave formal birth to the field, biblical theology has stood *over against* a variety of alternatives: over against strictly historical analysis (as when biblical theology stands for the good, appropriately theological way of reading Scripture), and over against skepticism on one hand or fundamentalism on the other. Biblical theology can stand for objective scholarship (when contrasted with "pneumatic" exegesis) or for subjectivity (when contrasted with interpretations by theologically disinterested scholars). Through all these transitions and conflicts, biblical theology has borne the marks of its polemical upbringing; since the Bible occupies uniquely desirable high ground in the theological battle zone, the discourses that seek to define biblical theology have continually been implicated in the very theological struggles they set out to resolve.[7] While every discipline may be able to tell a story of its birth from the fire of controversy, biblical theology shows a

4. J. P. Gabler, "On the Proper Distinction between Biblical and Dogmatic Theology and the Specific Objective of Each," in "J. P. Gabler and the Distinction between Biblical and Dogmatic Theology" (trans. John Sandys-Wunsch and Laurence Eldredge), *Scottish Journal of Theology* 33 (1980): 134.

5. Ibid., 136.

6. Ibid., 140.

7. That does not differentiate the present essay from its forebears, of course.

particularly long-lasting inclination to enlist, or to be drafted into, ever-new struggles for interpretive authority.

As biblical theology has grown in persistent conflict, so its adherents have tended to cast their rhetoric in terms of stark alternatives, some of which have attained the status of commonplaces. We have already observed the distinctions between biblical and dogmatic theology, between theology and religion; we can likewise cite distinctions between theology and history, between historical study of the Bible and pastoral or devotional study, between church and academy, between theological interpretation of Scripture and the history of early Christian religion. This pattern of refinement, of constriction, has contributed to an interpretive ethos within which the appropriate method of reading Scripture has been enclosed in order to fend off erroneous, misguided interpreters and to defend the correct approach to interpretation (always, of course, as we practice it) from the possibility that dangerous others might propose plausible readings of Scripture that undermine the stature of our legitimate interpretive modes.

If I were to devote more time to this element of my argument, I would explore the possibility that this flattening of discourse into polarities accelerated with the Reformation. When one may fairly expect that almost everyone is a Christian of roughly the same sort, acknowledging roughly the same structures of authority, then one will expect to see interpretive diversity concomitant with the catholicity of the church's teaching authority. Once Christian bodies defined themselves in opposition to the catholic tradition and cited the Bible as their primary criterion for that separation, each debater needed to erect an interpretive enclosure that sequestered the Bible on their home terrain. If I am right—and I emphasize that I make no claim to having plumbed the history of ecclesiastical controversy to back up this speculation—then as Protestant, Bible-identified bodies distinguish themselves from one another as well as from the catholic church, we might expect to find that the temperature in conflicts over biblical interpretation would also rise. As factional polemicists draft the (silent) Bible as a witness for partisan pleading, those who volunteer to tell us what the Bible really means show an increasing tendency toward minimizing the ambiguity of their evidence, toward maximizing the certainty of their conclusions.

The heat of ecclesiastical battle sacrifices nuance and precision to the cause of clear, simple, undebatable interpretive axioms. Controversy has not supplied the only force that drives biblical interpretation toward oversimplified polar extremes, however. Such forced choices correspond to the work most typically associated with biblical scholarship, namely, translation. However sophisticated one's theory of translation, however erudite one's grasp of the subtleties of Greek and Hebrew, Latin and Aramaic, when one prepares a translation one eventually must select a single expression in the target language to correspond to the expression in the original, ancient text.[8] A translator does not usually enjoy the liberty to translate the preface to Luke's Gospel like this:

> Inasmuch as many have set their hands, really sort of "tried," if you know what I mean, to compile, or put together, a narrative concerning the things that have taken place—really, "fulfilled" as you might say—among us, just as those who were eyewitnesses or who became ministers of the word handed them down to us, I too figured that after having followed everything precisely in order from the beginning, to write for you (most excellent Theophilus, which means "Godlover"), in order that you might learn (with overtones of "recognize") about the things you have been instructed, the certainty—or "you might learn the secure facts about what you've been taught."

Instead, the translator gets one unit of translated expression for each unit of text—and may indicate a few alternative readings only in footnotes. The translator's responsibility militates against ambivalence.

The habits that derive from translation shape the behavior of biblical interpreters, however, even when they are off translation duty. Our articles and essays promulgate the assumption that we are restricted, in our interpretive reading, to a *single best option* for apprehending any given passage from the Bible. Our exegetical arguments assert with vigor that now, at last, we have detected the decisive clue for clarifying interpretations that have eluded

8. The weight of this obligation falls especially on those who translate the Bible for major authorized editions; a translator's decision at Isa. 7:14 or Rom. 3:22 stands to affect theologies, liturgies, sermons, Sunday school lessons, and academic instruction in incalculably far-reaching ways.

two thousand years of close readers. We treat the biblical texts as cryptograms with a concealed key that, once discovered, will reveal a recognizably definite correct answer beyond any shadow of disagreement. Yet disagreements remain, demonstrating by their very durability that the mirage of textual determination has again retreated beyond the grasp of its pursuers, however brilliant, however faithful.

The paradigm that identifies all the work of biblical interpretation more or less forcefully with translation exercises further power over our imaginations to the extent that we assent to the conduit metaphor for language.[9] According to many figures of speech in English, words serve as vessels of meaning, containers or pipelines through which one pumps a meaning that one can distinguish from the pipe that contains it. We say, "I cannot *get into* that book" or "I could not get anything *out of* it"; we commonly define exegesis as "leading meaning *out of* the text" (as opposed to eisegesis: "reading meaning *into* the text"); we discuss interpretation as though meaning were within the words we exchange and as though we arrive at a successful understanding by siphoning the meaning out from its containment in words.

The combination of the translation paradigm, the conduit metaphor, and the ethos of interpretive competitiveness brings about a sort of *enclosure* of meaning. On the accounts of meaning that prevail in biblical theology, the church should permit only expert biblical scholars to determine the meaning of scriptural texts; these experts alone can correctly translate the best possible representation of the text's meaning into the language of the contemporary church. These scholars should study the text with no partiality, but if scholars communicate their interpretive conclusions in a way that does not evoke fervent affirmation of the gospel, then—apparently—something is *lacking*.

From Lack to Abundance

It is odd that anyone might perceive a lack in biblical interpretation, since the Bible must be one of the most interpreted

9. George Lakoff and Mark Johnson discuss the conduit metaphor in *Metaphors We Live By* (Chicago: University of Chicago Press, 1980), 127, 206.

texts in the world. The sheer staggering plenitude of biblical interpretation may to some extent account for scholars' artificial restriction on attention-worthy interpretations: if we wall off the sorts of interpretation to which we need to pay attention, we stand a slightly better chance of managing the flow of interpretations. We can carve out a space where the rules are clearer, the price of entry higher, the permitted gestures more limited. Once we have established this manageable domain of hermeneutical tidiness, we can name it "true biblical theology" or "legitimate theological interpretation" or what we will.

This safe zone of orderly biblical interpretation will remain, however, a fortified outpost isolated from the teeming flux of signification outside its secure walls. While cloistered biblical theologians debate the developmental pattern (or lack thereof) of the Pauline epistles, emergent-church congregations gather and grow, flourish and dwindle, worship and preach and argue. Theological interpretation thrives outside the walled precincts of academic biblical theology even as biblical theologians wonder how they lost their mojo.

The "enclosed" version of biblical theology aptly illustrates Michel de Certeau's analyses of reading and meaning.[10] De Certeau notes that intellectuals tend to establish informal regimes that regulate interpretive legitimacy; schools, public criticism, and lectures all inculcate the sense that there is a right way of reading to which the highly trained, sensitive interpreter is privy. These interpreters commonly represent such a restrictive gesture as necessary due to the nature of the text or the well-being of less expert readers (who might be misled without help from accredited scholars):[11]

> The use made of the book by privileged readers constitutes it as a secret of which they are the "true" interpreters. It interposes a frontier between the text and its readers that can be crossed only if one has a passport delivered by these official interpreters, who transform their own meaning (which is also a legitimate one)

10. Michel de Certeau, "Reading as Poaching," in *The Practice of Everyday Life* (trans. Steven Rendall; Berkeley: University of California Press, 1984), 165–76.

11. The staggering popular phenomenon of Dan Brown's *Da Vinci Code* testifies to the level of success that academic interpretive authority brings to bear on egregiously misleading interpretive claims: none at all.

into an orthodox "literality" that makes other (equally legitimate) readings either heretical (not "in conformity" with the meaning of the text) or insignificant (to be forgotten).[12]

De Certeau argues that readers are not bound by the conventions that privileged interpreters impose on the text; they are more like nomads than like a lockstep military formation.[13] Where biblical theologians try to seclude the meaning of Scripture in a closed field to which only the scholar has legitimate access, de Certeau reminds us that the Bible remains open to *un*authorized readers, who traverse the textual landscape as poachers or perhaps more fittingly as *gleaners*. While the privileged interpreters fastidiously redecorate the landscaping inside their gated community, unlicensed readers of the Bible continue to discover precious meaning in the dumpsters of academic criticism.[14]

In order to recuperate from what ails us, biblical theologians need to recognize that our experience of lack derives to a great extent from the self-imposed constraints on our discourse. Even if those constraints now seem obvious, natural, or theologically necessary, we may find that we simply cannot have the vibrant, profoundly biblical theology for which our essays lament at the same time that we stipulate a series of exclusions, qualifications, and preconditions for our discourse. If Augustine rightly asks, "what more liberal and more fruitful provision could God have made in regard to the Sacred Scriptures than that the same words might be understood in several senses?"[15] then the biblical theologian's task must more appropriately involve learning

12. De Certeau, "Reading as Poaching," 171.

13. A highly organized settled social group can look on nomadic wanderers as lawless and disorderly for disregarding the dominant group's conventions. Nonetheless, the nomadic group itself operates by a very strong array of social sanctions that simply differ from the ones that the dominant, settled group accepts as natural and necessary for civilized life.

14. This overwrought metaphor harks back to the point ably made by Carlos Mesters in *Defenseless Flower: A New Reading of the Bible* (trans. Francis McDonagh; Maryknoll, NY: Orbis, 1989), and advocated in James Dawsey, "The Lost Front Door into Scripture: Carlos Mesters, Latin American Liberation Theology, and the Church Fathers," *Anglican Theological Review* 72 (1990): 292–305.

15. Augustine, *On Christian Doctrine* 3.27.38 (trans. J. F. Shaw; Nicene and Post-Nicene Fathers 2); available at http://www.ccel.org/ccel/schaff/npnf102.html.

how to flourish in that divine abundance rather than devising conventions whose function is to attenuate the variety that God provides for our well-being.

For these purposes, the inherited mandates of biblical theology will persistently betray us. Though scholar after scholar proposes new and improved ways of doing the same interpretive thing, we will not thereby attain different results. A theological hermeneutic that develops out of the translation model, relies on the conduit metaphor, and relegates interpretive ventures to "either/or" characterizations will not equip its advocates to deal productively with semiotic abundance. A hermeneutic that respects the full catholicity of meaning needs to start by accepting abundance as a positive condition.

Coping Critically with Abundance

As the interpretive imaginations of so many readers have been formed decisively by the habits that *enclose* meaning, they recoil from the confusing prospect of semiotic abundance. Such readers adhere to this approach, which Stephen Fowl categorizes as "determinate interpretation"[16] and I as "integral hermeneutics,"[17] for plausible theological and philosophical reasons. If the familiar rules do not apply, these readers wonder whether one can say that texts mean whatever one likes. They wonder what criteria one might apply if the familiar criteria no longer determine legitimacy in interpretation.

These problems derive most of their force from the sheer unfamiliarity of critical interpretation outside the precincts of the cloister. As Fowl and I argue, however, interpreters have always applied criteria for evaluating interpretations, and—contrary to parodic representations of premodern hermeneutics—those criteria do not

16. Stephen E. Fowl, "Stories of Meaning," in *Engaging Scripture: A Model for Theological Interpretation* (Oxford: Blackwell, 1998), 32–61.

17. A. K. M. Adam, "Integral and Differential Hermeneutics," in *The Meanings We Choose: Hermeneutical Ethics, Indeterminacy, and the Conflict of Interpretations* (ed. Charles H. Cosgrove; Journal for the Study of the Old Testament Supplement 411; Edinburgh: T&T Clark, 2004), 24–38. Reprinted in A. K. M. Adam, *Faithful Interpretation* (Minneapolis: Fortress, forthcoming 2006).

simply amount to fanciful caprices.[18] The rule of faith, the spiritual senses of medieval interpretation, the reader's engagement with a network of other readers,[19] as well as various other aesthetic and ethical criteria, abound to ensure that interpretation does not float free of its accountability to standards. Indeed, even conventional critics tacitly appeal to a tremendous array of hermeneutical norms; the risk of arbitrariness dwindles markedly once one brings to conscious awareness the range of norms against which disciplined, faithful readers may check their interpretations.

The aforementioned allegorical approach to interpretation has long suffered the primary burden of modern deprecation. According to the Reformers, allegorical interpretation made of the text a wax nose "and wrest[ed] it this way and that way."[20] Yet Henri de Lubac's analysis of medieval exegesis underlines the extent to which medieval interpretation shows rich variety without arbitrariness, and recent studies bring to the foreground ways in which de Lubac's account of medieval interpretation might strengthen contemporary discourses of theological interpretation. David Steinmetz defends the hermeneutical superiority of medieval exegesis to contemporary interpretation;[21] Lewis Ayres offers an extended defense of allegorical interpretation as a soteriological exercise in cultivating a transformed, purified soul;[22] Margaret Adam suggests that the varied interpretive approaches of contemporary academic exegetes provide a complementary contemporary reflection of the fourfold interpretive

18. Frederic Farrar (*History of Interpretation* [London: Macmillan, 1886], 163–64) quotes John Milton as having said, "Whatsoever time or the heedless hand of blind chance hath drawn from of old to this present in her huge Dragnet, whether Fish or Seaweed, Shells or Shrubbs, unpicked, unchosen, those are the Fathers" (*Of Prelatical Episcopacy*). This outlook, left over from the conflict between ecclesiastical and academic authority, still prevails in many circles, though rarely expressed as deliciously.

19. Stephen E. Fowl and L. Gregory Jones expound this vital dimension of hermeneutics in *Reading in Communion* (Grand Rapids: Eerdmans, 1991).

20. William Tyndale, quoted by H. C. Porter in "The Nose of Wax: Scripture and the Spirit from Erasmus to Milton," *Transactions of the Royal Historical Society* 14 (1964): 155.

21. David Steinmetz, "The Superiority of Pre-critical Exegesis," *Theology Today* 37 (1980): 27–38.

22. Lewis Ayres, "The Soul and the Reading of Scripture: De Lubac's Doctrinal Implications," paper read to the Christian Theology and the Bible Section, Society of Biblical Literature Annual Meeting, Nov. 20, 2004.

schema of medieval interpreters;[23] and Graham Ward proposes *allēgoresis*, spiritual reading, as a mode of critical differentiation from interpretive approaches that restrict their attention to the material world, apart from the spiritual ramifications of textual meaning.[24] These represent only a thin selection from a growing body of scholarship that shows how we can take allegorical interpretation seriously as a contemporary possibility for critical reading.

These remain bounded by the captivity of our interpretive imagination to the representation of meaning in *words*. The world around us, however, teems with meanings expressed in nonverbal visual, auditory, and gestural signs. Indeed, the more one attends to the ways we encounter and reason through meaning in nonverbal understanding, the more parochial and limited the domain of words seems. To the extent that we suggest and infer meaning in countless nonverbal modes of expression, a hermeneutics that takes verbal communication as the definitive case of evoking and apprehending meaning inappropriately generalizes from the most formalized and unusual sphere of meaning-making to the more common and less specific spheres.[25]

Two sidenotes: First, this point marks one basis for my dissent from the way that theologians have appropriated speech-act theory's commendable advocacy of construing verbal and nonverbal communication together for philosophical and ethical evaluation; their version of speech-act theory still takes speech as the central focus of its analysis, tending to relegate "action" to the margin of meaningfulness. Second, the urgency of taking nonverbal meaning more seriously grows as an increasing proportion of communicators gain access to increasingly refined

23. Margaret Adam, "Beyond the Plain Sense: Why Frei When You Can de Lubac?" paper read to the Christian Theology and the Bible Section, Society of Biblical Literature Annual Meeting, Nov. 20, 2004.

24. Graham Ward, "Allegoria: Reading as a Spiritual Exercise," *Modern Theology* 15 (1999): 271–95.

25. Anthony C. Thiselton makes enthusiastic use of Wittgenstein's aphorism: "A picture held us captive" (*New Horizons in Hermeneutics: The Theory and Practice of Transforming Biblical Reading* [London: HarperCollins, 1992], passim). My point here turns Thiselton—but not Wittgenstein—upside down: The word has held us captive; not the theological Logos by which the second person of the Trinity is made known to us, but the prominence of verbal communication in our interpretive discourses.

tools for the production and transmission of audio and video expression online.[26]

Our hermeneutics should begin from the general phenomena of semiosis, of meaning-making. Once we have learned what we can say about meaning and interpretation in nonverbal domains, we can take on the special case of verbal communication with less risk that this outlying example of semiosis provides the key for all interpretive discourses.

In the context of theological hermeneutics, this attention to all the dimensions of meaning and communication obliges us to acknowledge that the windows that surround us exemplify biblical interpretation, that the worship for which this space is customarily used constitutes an exercise in biblical interpretation, that the architecture, the musical accompaniment or lack thereof, all these and more take part in the expansive, diverse practice of re-presenting the significance of the Bible in words, images, sounds, and gestures.

Biblical Theology as Signifying Practice

Hence, I propose that we think of biblical theology not on the model of translation, not on the basis of a conduit metaphor, but as a *signifying practice*. On this account, biblical theology would not involve just, or primarily, the verbal interpretation of verbal texts, but a way of living that deliberately enters into the ocean of signification that encompasses us and seeks a way to learn, to perpetuate, and to propagate the significance of the biblical proclamation. The signifying practice of biblical theology will include a great amount of textual interpretation, no doubt—but this practice will conduct its textual exploration toward the end of submitting visible, tangible, audible, *effectual* claims concerning the Bible's importance for our lives.

The term "signifying practice" came into currency through the work of Julia Kristeva, who deployed it in the context of analyzing two ways that language functions in a text. In the first

26. Cf. A. K. M. Adam, "This Is Not a Bible: Dispelling the Mystique of Words for the Future of Biblical Interpretation," in *New Paradigms for Bible Study: The Bible in the Third Millennium* (ed. Robert M. Fowler, Edith Blumhofer, and Fernando F. Segovia; New York: T&T Clark, 2004), 1–20.

function, language cooperates with the rules, conventions, and expectations that constitute conventional usage—the predictable elements that make satisfactory communication possible. The second function involves the ways that linguistic communication operates beyond or athwart rule-governed patterns of expression.[27] Kristeva characterizes the convergence of these functions as the way that all signifying takes place (even, as she allows, outside linguistic utterances).[28]

Subsequently, the Birmingham school of cultural criticism (particularly Stuart Hall and Dick Hebdige) took up the term to apply it not simply to the tension between linguistic system and specific utterances but also to the multifarious ways that people express themselves. In Hall's account, we participate in reciprocal social activities (including, but not limited to, speech and writing) in ways that affirm, amplify, and perpetuate meanings for our behavior; a particular integrated set of these words and actions constitutes a signifying practice, a complex tapestry of expression by which we assert the sorts of meaning by which we (and the culture around us) define our identities.[29] Hebdige applies this cultural semiotics to the ways that nondominant social groups define themselves over against the networks of meaning that prevail in the dominant social groups.[30] Thus gangstas, punks, goths, and various subcultures use their appearance, the sounds with which they make their presence audible, their distinct vernacular, the gestures by which they interact with one another and with outsiders—making meaning by the ways that they *signify*, in dress and music and speech and action.

27. I call signifying practice "the establishment and the countervailing of a sign system" from the glossary that Léon Roudiez appends to *Kristeva's Desire in Language: A Semiotic Approach to Literature and Art* (New York: Columbia University Press, 1980), 18; Roudiez quotes from *La traversée des signes*, without further specification.

28. Julia Kristeva, *The Kristeva Reader* (ed. Toril Moi; New York: Columbia University Press, 1986), 120–23, citing from *Revolution in Poetic Language*. Roland Barthes makes illuminating use of Kristeva's distinction between phenotext and genotext in his essay "The Grain of the Voice," in *Image-Music-Text* (trans. Stephen Heath; New York: Hill & Wang, 1977), 179–89.

29. Stuart Hall, ed., *Representation: Cultural Representations and Signifying Practices* (London: Sage, 1997), 15–64, esp. 28–29.

30. Dick Hebdige, *Subculture: The Meaning of Style* (London: Routledge, 1979).

As a provocative digression, I will here propose in one paragraph my working axioms of semiotics. First, *everything signifies*: our dress, our posture, our tone, our stride; in a Word-created world, everything signifies. Second, signification cannot be controlled. We often attempt to control signifying under the rule of intention ("I did not intend to scandalize you, so it is not my responsibility if you are hurt by what I did"). The rule of intention has long been known to lead to hell, though, and no other mode of policing signification has proved more effective. If I wear an orange jacket through the wrong neighborhood on Saint Patrick's Day, that will signify, whether I intend it to or not, and the significance may be enforced with sanctions that pay no respect to refined arguments about the nature of human intention or the legitimacy of reader-oriented interpretation. If my word or gesture hurts you unintentionally, you are still injured regardless, and I am complicit in that injury. Third, then, there is no ethic intrinsic to signification—the signifying Spirit blows where it will, and we know not whence it comes or whither it goes—but only in our practices of expression and apprehension. We interpret significance in particular ways, and we speak and gesture in certain ways, relying on provisional expectations and conventions. Those derive their sanction, however, not from the nature of signification, but from our understanding of how we ought to live in a world that is more complex than we are capable of controlling. As surfers, we do not control the waves of signification, but we negotiate their flux, riding forces that we cannot command.

The benefits of adopting the terminology of "signifying practice" for biblical theology are manifold. First, when we frame biblical theology as signifying practice, we point *away from* an exclusively verbal model of signification and expression toward a model that encompasses all our activity. We break out of the circle of texts interpreting texts, into a world in which every sphere of human action expresses our biblical interpretations and invites critical analysis. Biblical interpretations formulated as stained-glass windows or paintings, as oratorios or praise songs, as eucharistic prayers, or indeed as ecstatic pentecostal utterance take a coherent place in our reflection on the theological meanings of our Bible. Moreover, when we take up biblical theology as a signifying practice, we direct our attention toward ways that our lived practice as biblical interpreters constitutes an ongoing interpretation of the Bible. Since the God of the Bible (in the varied forms in which Christians and Jews receive it) expresses especially vivid interest in how one orders one's life, and since most biblical theologians profess some sort of allegiance to this God who was made known to Israel, to whom Jesus of Nazareth pointed as uniquely good and holy, we have strong reasons *as biblical theologians* not to separate our lived interpretive practice from our academic, verbal interpretive deliberation. The segregation of ethics or homiletics or liturgics from biblical interpretation dissolves into a critical study of the ways that particular expressions and practices fittingly or inappropriately bespeak the meanings we infer from biblical precedents.

Once we adjust our expectations to regard biblical theology as a signifying practice rather than as puzzle in an arcane code, pieces of the theological vocation that have fallen apart come together again in gratifying and challenging ways. Interpretive disagreement no longer requires that we slug it out until one reader's proposal shows all others to be inferior; indeed, we must expect disagreement as an authentic representation of biblical theologies that emerge from divergent contexts, represented by divergent practitioners; just as any two harpsichordists will perform a shared score differently, so two biblical theologians will perform their shared scriptural score differently.[31] The biblical theologian studies Scripture for the cues for his or her particular performance, imbibes the characteristic directions and gestures, the prohibitions and requirements, and improvises a biblical response to the congregation, the pastoral situation, the social circumstances he or she confronts.[32] Some degree of innovation

31. I believe Frances Young to have brought the matter of "performance" to the seminar table of biblical hermeneutics in *The Art of Performance: Toward a Theology of Holy Scripture* (London: Darton, Longman & Todd, 1990); published in the U.S. under the title *Virtuoso Theology: The Bible and Interpretation* (Cleveland: Pilgrim, 1993). See also, however, Nicholas Lash's pivotal article "Performing the Scriptures," in *Theology on the Way to Emmaus* (London: SCM, 1986), 37–46 (originally published in *The Furrow* in 1982), indeed, all of part 2 of *Theology on the Way to Emmaus*.

32. The literature on performance, improvisation, and ethics has grown dramatically; the central work, for now, is Samuel Wells's *Improvisation: The Drama of Christian Ethics* (Grand Rapids: Brazos, 2004). Nicholas Cook proposes an illuminating discussion of the relation of musical improvisation to a score in "Prompting Performance: Text, Script, and Analysis in Bryn Harrison's *être-temps*," *Music Theory Online* 11 (2005), http://www.societymusictheory.org/mto/

will prove intolerable to us, and we will resist and oppose it; other degrees of innovation will seem appropriate to our text, and we will welcome the fresh light they shed on Scripture.

Our exemplifications, our embodiments of biblical theology, will always in some respects depart from their biblical precedents, so that we cannot *simply* assert that our practice fulfills the mandates of our biblical score. Our practice of biblical theology will express our sense of Scripture more or less faithfully, more or less recognizably, and observers of our practice will assess it differently depending on their own apprehension of biblical theology. This befits the Bible, which itself is not monophonic, but comprises a tremendous variety of material for us to emphasize, defer, mute, harmonize, and resolve in ways that themselves always change; in the words of Hans Urs von Balthasar, "Truth is symphonic."[33] Those of us who are Anglicans may appropriate this criterion to the instruction in Article XX of our Articles of Religion, which stipulates that the church may not "so expound one place of Scripture, that it be repugnant to another." Confronted by possibly ugly perplexities in the score of our performance, we may not simply adopt one passage and reject the other, citing one passage as the basis for *negating* the other. Instead, the articles instruct us to seek the way of reading by which our exposition resolves apparent discord into a more profound, unexpected harmony.

In order soundly to *signify* Scripture, we need to know the Bible well, studying the Bible steadily and faithfully. In contradistinction to the ways that many prominent biblical theologians have framed their definitions and axioms, that entails studying the canonical biblical text. While speculation about precanonical sources may nuance our appreciation of the canon, Q is not a substitute for Matthew (as Watson suggests in chapter 4). Similarly, we have

---

issues/mto.05.11.1/mto.05.11.1.cook_frames.html. For guidance on such matters, I depend on instruction from musicians, but the relation between interpretation and musical improvisation has captured the imaginations of several interesting expositors: not only Wells, but also Trevor Bechtel, "How to Eat Your Bible," *Conrad Grebel Review* 21 (2003): 81–87; Stephen Barton, "New Testament Interpretation as Performance," *Scottish Journal of Theology* 52 (1999): 179–208; and pianist/pastor Bill Carter. I suspect, though I have no textual evidence, that Charles Cosgrove's perceptive reflections on the relation of Scripture to theology and ethics have been informed by his experience playing jazz trombone.

33. Hans Urs von Balthasar, *Truth Is Symphonic* (trans. Graham Harrison; San Francisco: Ignatius, 1987).

much to learn from *post*canonical commentary, particularly commentary from the saints who wrote during the time (described in Fowl's essay in chapter 2) when *sacra doctrina* comprised all the theological specializations, but commentary does not substitute for the Bible. Perhaps above all, the signifying practice of biblical theology depends on our reading Scripture together, in conjunction with our lives of discipleship and worship. By hearing the word together, by responding to the word together, by conversing about the word together, we encounter and embody at least a beginning measure of the richness that arises when different servants of the same word practice together.

Thus, our worship—in a certain sense, the signifying practice of biblical theology par excellence—best serves our vocation when we tone down the liturgical expression of *ourselves* and devote our energies to focusing attention on a gospel that we did not invent, in ways that direct attention away from us, away from our ingenuity, away from the urgent messages we need to convey, away from our resourcefulness, and toward the God whom we praise. Romano Guardini advises: "The priest of the late nineteenth century who said, 'We must organize the procession better; we must see to it that the singing and praying are done better' [should have rather] asked himself quite a different question: how can the act of walking become a religious act, a retinue for the Lord progressing through his land, so that an epiphany may take place?"[34]

Our processional *walking*, however, must take our lives, fortified by the ritual expression of orchestrated praise, outward into a dissonant and disordered world. As biblical theologians, we endeavor to recognize God's ways at work around us and to lend our lived testimony to strengthening, making more nearly visible and audible, the gospel way. We shape our lives after the patterns that we discern in Scripture, so that others may see our good works and give glory to God. We take up the imitation of Christ, the imitation of Mary and Moses, of Abigail and James, so that their significance resonates in the paths we walk. We study Scripture here not simply to learn a set of rules we must follow but also to learn a repertoire of roles we enact. And by

34. A multinested citation: Guardini as cited by Mark Searles in "Liturgy as Hermeneutics," as cited by Graham Hughes, *Worship as Meaning* (Cambridge: Cambridge University Press, 2003), 39.

taking up the whole of our lives as a signifying practice of biblical theology, we make ourselves accountable to our neighbors.
Without entrusting our signifying practice to the loving criticism
of our sisters and brothers, we fall prey to the fallacy of assuming
that we signify only what we intend. If we share our lives with
reliable friends, their good examples can encourage our persis-
tence in prayer and service, and they can help catch us when our
intentions no longer match what our lives signify.

So—to conclude—our friends make us better biblical theologians, and our congregational worship makes us better biblical
theologians, and the wisdom of the saints makes us better biblical
theologians. Thus the following litany of thanksgivings is no idle
rhetorical convention but a necessary affirmation that all that is true
has come to us as a *gift*: thanks to my children and parents, who have
accommodated my busyness and abstractedness over many years;
to friends, who have put up with my limitations and opened for me
a path toward greater wisdom; to my students, who teach me more
every time I *dare* stand up before them; to the schools and founda-
tions that have supported and encouraged my studies; to Margaret,
in every way my better half; and to the congregations in which it
has been my privilege to serve. All of you have played a decisive
role in my understanding of ministry and biblical theology and of
how much we stand to benefit from allowing these two activities
to shape each other more actively and deliberately.[35] Since we have
been so graciously surrounded by so great a cloud of witnesses, we
squander our energy if we construct a hothouse of artificial scarcity
within which to sit in splendid disciplinary isolation, bemoaning
our lack; instead, as biblical theologians we process confidently,
with angels and archangels and all the company of heaven, into the
abundant flux of meaning that surrounds and suffuses us, practic-
ing at every turn the harmony, the diligence, and the gratitude by
which our biblical theology testifies to the grace of Christ.

35. I owe more specific thanks also to Lynette Sweet, Laura Jackson, and
Michelle Warriner-Bolt, who engaged in a seminar on Meaning and Ministry
with me in the Michaelmas Term of 2004; to Laura and Micah Jackson, for help
in attaining perspective on the argument at which this essay aims; to Nathaniel
Adam, for conversation about musical improvisation and textuality; and to David
Aune and the Colloquium on Christian and Jewish Antiquity at the University
of Notre Dame, for a generous invitation to talk through some of these issues
beforehand.

2

The Importance of a Multivoiced Literal Sense of Scripture

The Example of Thomas Aquinas

Stephen E. Fowl

Recently, we Episcopalians have been arguing over a variety of issues. Many of the voices in these arguments claim to take Scripture literally. Other voices argue that it is impossible to take all of Scripture literally with any consistency. Thus, even those who claim to do so are unwittingly selective in the elements they take literally and those they do not. For the most part, both sides use the term *literal* in its prevailing modern sense of having only one meaning. Historically, this is not what most Christians prior to the seventeenth century meant by taking Scripture literally or by attending to the literal sense of Scripture. One of my arguments is that we would do well to recover this premodern understanding of the literal sense and that the best place to start such a recovery is with the work of Thomas Aquinas. Now, I am not a Thomas scholar. My primary interest in him is as a biblical commentator and theologian. I am not committed to defending everything the Angelic Doctor ever wrote. On this set of issues, however, I happen to think Thomas gets things right.

I propose to do three things here in the course of this essay. First, I will describe briefly what Thomas means when he talks about the literal sense of Scripture. Although he was not unique in emphasizing the importance of the literal sense of Scripture, Thomas was in a decided minority in his day.[1] Within Thomas's vast corpus of writing there are actually very few places where he discusses the literal sense of Scripture in any real detail. This may sound surprising considering that Thomas spent the majority of his academic career lecturing and commenting on Scripture. At the very least, this indicates that Thomas did not have much interest in articulating a general hermeneutic that could be applied always and everywhere. This is not to say that Thomas shunned interpretive disputes over Scripture. On the contrary, his scriptural commentaries devote a great deal of space to adjudicating between competing interpretive options. Thomas will often rule some interpretations to be inadequate or mistaken. Nevertheless, Thomas will also recognize that any particular passage of Scripture may legitimately support a diversity of interpretations, each of which counts as the literal sense of that passage.

After outlining Thomas's views on the literal sense, I will try to show how this works in practice. That is, I will try to show how Thomas's account of a multifaceted literal sense of Scripture works itself out in his interpretation of a particular biblical passage, John 1:1.

Finally, having laid out Thomas's account of a multifaceted literal sense of Scripture and then illustrated it in practice, I want to ask why it was important for Thomas to hold such a view of scriptural interpretation. Moreover, I want to explore the commitments and ideas that underwrote Thomas's views on the literal sense of Scripture. As I mentioned, Thomas says very little of what we might call a theoretical nature about the many-faceted literal sense of Scripture. He says even less about

1. Nicholas of Lyra and Hugh of Saint Victor are often cited as those who also urged the priority of the literal sense of Scripture.

the importance of holding this view. Thus, my remarks in this part of the essay will be based in part on what Thomas does say and in part on what I think one can fairly infer from Thomas's broader theological views. Thus, some of these remarks will, I hope, be Thomas-like, even if not explicitly stated in Thomas's own words.

To anticipate my argument here somewhat let me say that Thomas thinks that a many-faceted literal sense of Scripture is needed because of the Christian doctrine of God; because it helps to foster and maintain Christian community and, in particular, the communion of saints; because of his views about the dignity of Scripture and the place of Scripture in Christian life and thought; and last, but by no means least, because of his concern that his students and all people grow into an ever deeper friendship with God. Thus, to reveal my punch line here, to the extent that we today share in these views about God, the church, Scripture, theological study, and the proper end of human life—and we should share in them—we should also consider holding a similar notion of a many-sided literal sense of Scripture.

In many respects, my argument simply furthers other arguments I have made for several years now, often in direct engagement with my fellow essayists. The argument in a nutshell is that theology and ecclesiology should drive scriptural hermeneutics, not the other way around.

Thomas's Literal Sense of Scripture

Thomas lived from 1224 to 1274. Most of the material I consider in this essay was written between 1252 and 1267. During the first part of this period Thomas was professor at the University of Paris. He was then called to teach and direct the studies of students in the Roman province of the Dominicans.[2]

If one's exposure to Thomas and his work is limited, one probably thinks of him primarily as a medieval philosopher and theologian, the author of that very large and hard to manage

2. For more details of Thomas's life, see the full and very readable biography by J.-P. Torrell, *Saint Thomas Aquinas*, vol. 1: *The Person and His Work* (trans. Robert Royal; rev. ed.; Washington, DC: Catholic University of America Press, 2005).

Summa theologiae. This is not incorrect. It is important, however, to nuance this point in several ways. First, for Thomas and his contemporaries, theology was not a fragmented discipline comprised of systematic theology, church history, liturgy, and biblical studies. Although one might study any one of these topics, they were all seen as part of something unified called theology or, to use Thomas's term, *sacra doctrina*, frequently translated "sacred doctrine." Thus, in the words of Thomas Prügl, "'Sacred doctrine,' therefore, was not restricted to any one of the theological specializations familiar to us today. Rather it was seen more broadly, as the process of transmission of saving knowledge originating in God and reaching humankind through church doctrine, Scripture and theology."[3] Because of this it is better to follow some modern scholars, including my colleague Fritz Bauerschmidt, who translate *sacra doctrina* as "holy teaching." This translation usefully reminds us that the aim of studying holy teaching was not simply to grow in our knowledge of God, and thus learn the proper shape of holiness, but so that one would also grow in holiness. Thus, the study of theology had as its end the deepening of the student's life with God.

Conceiving theology or holy teaching in this way requires one to view Scripture as the foremost of God's providential gifts to humans. Because Scripture uniquely reveals the truth about God, the world, and God's relationship to the world, it enables all subsequent theological work to get off the ground (see *Summa theologiae* 1.Q. 1. arts. 8–9 on the need for revelation). As a professor, or Master of the Sacred Page, Thomas's primary task was to lecture on and explain Scripture. Moreover, as a member of the Dominican order, the Order of Preachers, Thomas proclaimed Scripture on a regular basis. Even in his *Summa theologiae* it is difficult to read very far without coming across a scriptural citation or allusion. Indeed, through the miracle of modern technology we now know that in the *Summa theologiae* there are 5.44 scriptural quotations for every 1,000 words and that scriptural quotations make up 39 percent of all quotations in the *Summa*

---

3. T. Prügl, "Thomas Aquinas as Interpreter of Scripture," in *The Theology of Thomas Aquinas* (ed. R. van Nieuwenhove and J. Wawrykow; Notre Dame: University of Notre Dame Press, 2005), 386.

theologiae, by far the most.[4] Thus, to call Thomas a theologian is first and foremost to call him a biblical theologian.[5]

If my account of Thomas's deep commitment to Scripture is accurate, and if Thomas believes that any particular passage of Scripture might have several literal senses, then one's thinking might well be running along the following lines: if theology and theological argument must be founded on Scripture, then it would seem that for Scripture to have many possible senses would invite confusion. It is precisely this concern that Thomas takes up in the beginning of his *Summa theologiae*. By way of answering this question, Thomas begins by injecting a variety of refinements.

First, he distinguishes between the spiritual and the literal senses of Scripture. The spiritual senses of Scripture treat passages of Scripture and the things referred to in Scripture as signs of other things. Thus, things witnessed to in the Old Testament can point to things witnessed to in the New Testament. Things that point to the Christ can be used to point out things for us to imitate. Things that point to the future can indicate the ways in which we ought to guide our hope in the present. These spiritual senses are often called the allegorical, the moral, and the anagogical, but designating them this way is not that important. It is much more important to understand that these spiritual senses depend on one's ability to discern similarities between things mentioned in the Old Testament and things mentioned in the New Testament, between Jesus's deeds and our own, between our final end and our present situation, and so on. Reading for the spiritual senses is a disciplined practice of discerning connections. Growing in our abilities to see such connections and similarities is important to our growth in holiness. As a result,

4. Wilhelmus G. B. M. Valkenberg, *Words of the Living God: Place and Function of Holy Scripture in the Theology of St. Thomas Aquinas* (Leuven: Peeters, 2000), 75.

5. For example, in regard to Thomas's comments on John 1:16–18, Matthew Levering notes that Thomas cites three of the four Gospels, eleven of the twenty-seven books of the New Testament, and thirteen books of the Old Testament. He concludes, "As a resource for reading the Bible canonically (employing the analogy of faith) and with attention to the patristic interpreters, Aquinas' exegesis is exemplary." See M. Levering, "Reading John with St. Thomas Aquinas," in *Aquinas on Scripture: An Introduction to His Biblical Commentaries* (ed. T. Weinandy, D. Keating, and J. Yocum; Edinburgh: T&T Clark, 2005), 101.

there was a great deal of emphasis on spiritual interpretation of Scripture in Thomas's day. Learning to read Scripture spiritually was essential for the formation of priests and monks, for whom most of the scriptural commentaries of the time were written.

Without denigrating this practice, Thomas wants students to understand two important things about the spiritual senses of Scripture. First, because they depend on the discernment of similarities between things, similarities that may change over time and may not be easy to discern in the first place, there is an inherent instability in the spiritual senses of Scripture. This instability makes the spiritual senses unsuitable as the basis for theology or theological argument. Second, Thomas claims that any edifying spiritual interpretation of Scripture must have a basis in the literal sense of some scriptural text. Thus, in answer to the claim that a plurality of senses of Scripture invites confusion, Thomas first distinguishes the spiritual from the literal senses of Scripture.

It would appear, then, that Thomas deals with this question by noting that although the spiritual senses of a passage may be many and varied, the literal sense is single, stable, and a sufficient basis for theology. This, however, is not the case.

What is the literal sense of Scripture? On this Thomas's answer is disarmingly simple. The "literal sense of Scripture is what the author of Scripture intends to be understood by the words that are written."[6] Here, however, things take a bit of a twist. Thomas holds that the primary author of Scripture is God, or more precisely the Holy Spirit. The human authors under the Spirit's inspiration are significant, though secondary in this respect.[7] The Spirit is capable of understanding all things and intending more by the words of Scripture than humans could ever fully grasp (*De quodlibet* Q. 7 art. 6.1 ad 5). This means that believers should not be surprised to find that there may be many

6. Mark F. Johnson, "Another Look at the Plurality of the Literal Sense," *Medieval Philosophy and Theology* 2 (1992): 119.

7. Indeed, Thomas is also willing to grant that, under the Spirit's inspiration, the human authors of Scripture may have intended several things by their words: "It is not inconceivable that Moses and the other authors of the Holy Books were given to know the various truths that men would discover in the text, and that they expressed them under one literary style, so that each truth is the sense intended by the author" (*De potentia* Q. 4 art. 1.8).

manifestations of the literal sense of a passage. Here is what Thomas says in the *Summa theologiae*: "Since the literal sense is that which the author intends, and since the author of Holy Scripture is God, Who by one act comprehends everything all at once in God's understanding, it is not unfitting, as Augustine says [*Confessions* 12], if many meanings [*plures sensus*] are present even in the literal sense of a passage of Scripture" (*Summa theologiae* 1.Q. 1. art. 10).

If the aim here is to eliminate confusion and distortion in Christian thinking, the sort of multifaceted literal sense that Thomas advocates here and elsewhere would appear to be a recipe for disaster. This is not the case, however. To help see why, I will look at what Thomas's commitment to a multifaceted literal sense of Scripture looks like when he turns to offering theological commentary on a biblical text.

Thomas's Literal Sense in Practice: John 1:1

The familiar opening of John's Gospel provides a good example of Thomas's theological commentary: "In the beginning was the Word." Thomas begins his comments with a series of reflections on "the Word" (Latin *verbum*).[8] He is at pains to show what he takes to be the foundational truth of this passage: the Word is to be identified with the second person of the Trinity, the Word is co-eternal with the Father and fully divine. He does this with care and precision. Having already established what he takes to be the crucial theological assertion of this passage, he turns to explore the phrase *in the beginning* (*in principio* in Latin).

Thomas notes that the word *principium* has many meanings. As he sees it, however, they all have some commonalities: "Since the word *principium* implies a certain order of one thing to another, one can find a *principium* in all those things which have an order" (36). He then notes various types of order: quantities of things, units of time, a process with a start and an end, and so forth. He then asks: "Considering these various ways of using the term, we now ask how *principium* is used here when it says 'in

8. The following citations are from Thomas's *Commentary on the Gospel of John* (ed. and trans. J. Weisheipl and F. Larcher; vol. 1; Albany: Magi, 1980).

the beginning was the Word' [*in principio erat Verbum*]" (37). This procedure is quite common in modern scholarly commentaries: the commentator surveys the possible ways in which a word can be used and then offers a judgment about how the word is used in the specific context of particular verse.

Thomas first argues that there are three possible ways of taking this phrase. In the first, *principium* refers to the Son: "Taking *principium* in this way, we should understand the statement 'in the beginning was the Word' as though he were saying, 'The Word was in the Son,' so the sense would be: The Word himself is the *principium*, principle, in the sense in which life is said to be 'in' God, when this life is not something other than God" (37). As Thomas says, this way of reading *principium* indicates something like the Word was in the Son.[9] This is not to indicate a distinction between Son and Word. Rather, this reading treats the Word as the rational pattern and vivifying power of creation and locates this within the Son. Thus, according to Thomas, Christ can be identified in 1 Corinthians 1:24 as the power and wisdom of God. In this way the identity of Word with the Son is not as a separable attribute of the Son, but as identical with the Son.

The second way is to understand *principium* in terms of the Father, who is not only the principle of creatures but also of the divine processions. This way of reading *principium* leads to a reading of "in the beginning was the Word" that affirms that "the Son was in the Father." This reading anticipates Jesus's claim later in John 14:10: "I am in the Father and the Father is in me."[10]

Finally, *principium* can be taken to signify a temporal beginning. In this way "in the beginning was the Word" asserts that the Word was before all things, that the Word is eternal. Thomas invokes the traditional christological reading of Proverbs 8:23 in support of this.[11]

Thomas concludes this discussion by summarizing the three positions: "And thus the first explanation asserts the causality of the Word; the second explanation affirms the consubstantiality of the Word with the Father who utters the Word; and the third

9. Origen and Chrysostom are cited by Thomas as examples of this view.
10. Origen and Augustine are cited by Thomas as examples of this view.
11. Basil and Hilary are cited by Thomas as examples of this view.

explanation affirms the co-eternity of the Word" (38). Each position and its proponents are clearly laid out. At this point, modern commentaries offer their punch line when the commentator tells which of these possibilities is correct. Thomas, however, expresses no preference for one possibility over the other. He treats them all as literal senses of John 1:1.

This might lead us to ask something like this: Given that Thomas treats each of these interpretations of John 1:1 as the literal sense of the text, was he right in doing so? Of course, everything here hinges on what one means by "right." That is, by what standard are these considered to be true versions of the literal sense of John 1:1? To answer that question I need to turn briefly to the other significant place in Thomas's writings where he discusses the literal sense of Scripture a bit more fully.

Thomas gives his fullest account of a multifaceted literal sense of Scripture in *De potentia*, a work discussing disputed questions concerning God's power. The relevant discussion arises from Thomas's attempt to negotiate an interpretive dispute over Genesis 1:2: "And the earth was formless and void." The question at stake here is whether the creation of formless matter preceded the creation of formed things and whether such formation occurred all at once or little by little. While we do not think in terms of formed and unformed matter today, over the course of many centuries the most sophisticated intellects in the West thought in these terms. Addressing this issue as it relates to creation was perhaps the equivalent of engaging contemporary physics and cosmology today. In adjudicating this issue Thomas is faced with two different accounts of Genesis 1:2. On the one hand is Augustine's view that God created the world in a single instant. On the other hand is the view held by Basil, Gregory of Nyssa, and Ambrose (among others) that creation occurred successively in time and required the successive creation of unformed matter.

It is less important that we come to sympathize with the metaphysics and physics of each view. It is important, however, that we understand that each side saw their position as consistent with the proper way to interpret Genesis 1:2. In the course of arguing that both should be considered the literal sense of Genesis 1:2, Thomas says more about the nature of the literal sense. He notes that each interpretation affirms that God is the Creator of all things. Each view does no violence to the text and its context as Thomas sees it. Neither view has Scripture assert something demonstrably false. Thus, he says one should not "constrict the meaning of a text of Scripture in such a way as to preclude other truthful meanings that can, without destroying the context, be fitted to Scripture."[12] Given this, Thomas counts each view as the literal sense of Genesis 1:2.

This gives more criteria for adjudicating the question of whether an interpretation should count as one of the literal senses of that text. The account of the literal sense from the *Summa theologiae* tied the literal sense to the intention of Scripture's divine author. We know that the Spirit is capable of intending far more things by a passage of Scripture than we could ever fully comprehend. At the same time, we would be safe in claiming that any interpretation that demanded that Scripture teach something demonstrably false could not have been intended by the Spirit, who is, after all, the Spirit of truth. So, any assertion that was demonstrably false could not reflect the author's intention and would do violence to the context of a passage.[13] While hoping to eliminate falsehood, Thomas is also very concerned that we not confine a text's ability to say many true things. One "should not confine the meaning of a passage of Scripture under one sense so as to exclude any other interpretations that are actually or possibly true that do not violate the context" (*De potentia* Q. 4 art. 1.8). Thus, Thomas claims here that we should neither take falsehood to be the literal sense nor confine the meaning of a text of Scripture to the extent that we exclude other truthful claims.

Of course, that is not much of a limitation. One can say all sorts of true things about God and the world that are not obviously related to any specific scriptural text. Thus, if we were to go back to John 1:1 and the term *principium*, we would not expect Thomas to take the truth that God loves us and assert that this truth is part of the literal sense of "in the beginning was the Word." The claim is true, but tying its truth to the words of John 1:1 does violence to the context of the passage. This is

12. Translated by Johnson, "Another Look at the Plurality," 127. There is a parallel statement in *Scriptum super libros sententiarum* 2.12.1.2 corp.

13. In addition, in *De potentia* Q. 4.1 Thomas notes that such an interpretation would offer ammunition to the enemies of the faith.

the other judgment that Thomas brings in here in *De potentia*. Interpreters should not include falsehood or preclude interpretations that teach truthful meanings that do not do violence to the context.

Unfortunately, Thomas does not appear to give much more direction on what may count as contextual violence. It is clear that this is in large measure a judgment call, but it is not an uninformed judgment call. We can see this by looking at factors that informed Thomas's judgment. From his treatment of John 1:1 it is clear that all of the literal interpretations he offers have support from holy interpreters from the past, such as Origen, Augustine, and Basil. However, one should not think that Thomas will simply accept an interpretation just because it has a patristic pedigree. He is quite capable of offering critical and corrective judgments of Origen, Basil, and Augustine when he thinks they have made interpretive mistakes. Unless he can detect the mistake, however, he tends to grant that the exemplary interpreters of the past did not do violence to the context of a passage. Thus, prior unfalsified attestation by one of the church's exemplary interpreters would yield a judgment that a reading did not violate the context of a passage.

In discussing each of the literal senses of John 1:1 Thomas readily makes intertextual connections between biblical passages such as 1 Corinthians 1:24; John 14:10; Proverbs 8:23; and others. It would, therefore, also appear that for Thomas the context of a passage is its location within the canonical Scriptures as a whole. So the context of John 1:1 would be much larger than the linguistic units immediately surrounding the verse. Thus, if an interpretation of John 1:1 expressly contradicted another passage of Scripture, Thomas would think that such an interpretation did violence to the context of John 1:1.

Let me summarize where things stand with our exploration of Thomas and the literal sense of Scripture. First, Thomas is committed to the priority of the literal sense above the spiritual senses when it comes to the relationships between Scripture and Christian faith and practice. Second, a passage's literal sense is that which the author of Scripture, the Holy Spirit, intends. Because the Spirit intends more in a verse than we can ever comprehend, it should not surprise us that there may be many literal senses of a text. The literal sense of a passage must not require

Scripture to teach falsehoods. It must be true or potentially true and not do violence to the context of a passage.

Thomas's View of Scriptural Interpretation

Even with this clarification of Thomas's notion of the multifaceted literal sense of Scripture, one may still think that the idea of Scripture having a many-voiced literal sense is rubbish, a particularly bad version of medieval hairsplitting. In order to convince us that this may be a notion worth considering, I want to explore the connections between Thomas's views about the literal sense of Scripture and his views about Scripture and its role in the life of believers, about God, about the communion of saints, and about theological education. These views are all connected with each other to some degree. Thus, I am trying to entice us believers into accepting Thomas's views about the literal sense of Scripture by finding that we share a set of other commitments and convictions with him that implicate us in his views about the literal sense.

Because the points I want to make here are interconnected, it is hard to know where to begin. For example, it would be important to mention at the outset that unlike some contemporary Christians, Thomas does not think of scriptural study as an end in itself. God has provided Scripture to the church so that we believers might be drawn ever closer to our true end: ever deeper friendship with God. This is what we have been created for; this is God's most heartfelt desire for us. All that we do as believers should be directed toward enhancing our movement toward that end. This is a point about Scripture, but it is also a point about God and about the proper ends of human life. In other words, we must keep a variety of things in view.

With that in mind, I want to begin by examining what might be called Thomas's doctrine of Scripture. Really, however, doctrine might be too systematic a term for the collection of views that Thomas either explicitly holds or can be presumed to have held based on his other views. Since Thomas treats Scripture and its literal sense as the foundation for all subsequent arguments about "holy teaching," what sort of foundation is this? Thomas Prügl states it well: "The purpose of Thomas's exegesis is not the establishment of dogmatic proof based on Scripture. It aims rather at an agreement or a correspondence between Scripture and the doctrine of faith; or as he himself put it, the continuation of *manifestatio veritatis* by interpreting the fixed form of this manifestation."[14] In this respect, our theology really becomes a form of exegetical exercise as we learn to conform our ideas or bring them into fitting agreement with Scripture. In Thomas's eyes this is simply what Paul means when he advocates bringing every thought captive to Christ (2 Cor. 10:5). Scripture is a gift that enables us to fulfill Paul's admonition. If we come to share this view, everything that we can see, think, or do could be comprehended by Scripture.

This is because Thomas assumes that Scripture is the most important of God's providential gifts for ordering, understanding, and making the world accessible to humans. In this light, the Scripture presents a unified narrative through which people could develop unified, coherent views of the world that would allow God to bring them to their proper end of ever deeper friendship with God. Because the world is complex, sometimes ambiguous, and regularly subject to change, a multifaceted literal sense of Scripture will be a much more successful way of comprehending God, the world, others, and all that falls between in ways that enhance our prospects of being brought to our proper end in God.

If there can only be one literal sense to each passage of Scripture then it will become difficult if not impossible for Scripture to function as the lenses through which we order and comprehend things, including God. There are two reasons for this. First, Scripture understood in this way will lack the capacity to address the ever changing complexity of our world and of our lives. Second, it will become difficult if not impossible to avoid the charge that Scripture teaches something demonstrably false. To see this, let us go back to the issue of Genesis 1, though not to the question of formed versus unformed matter. If there is only one literal sense of the creation account in Genesis 1, then Christians are likely to be committed to the idea that the world was created in six days. Although there may be some flexibility in the notion and duration of these days, it is hard to avoid the conclusion

14. Prügl, "Thomas Aquinas as Interpreter of Scripture," 403.

that Scripture is going to be in danger of asserting falsehood. Thomas's view of the literal sense would enable him not only to address controversies surrounding formed and unformed matter, but he could also, given sufficient training, account for the Big Bang or other contemporary scientific views without compromising the literal sense of Genesis 1:1.

In addition, Thomas's doctrine of God is implicated in his views of Scripture and its literal sense. The very presence of Scripture is the result of God's desire to enter into friendship with humans. It is both God's most definitive overture and God's continuing response to our faith as it seeks both deeper understanding and truer love of God. Because God loves us and desires to draw us into an ever deeper friendship, God, through the Spirit, speaks a multiplicity of meanings into the literal sense of Scripture. In this way, God invites believers to deepen their knowledge of and friendship with God through repeated and ongoing engagement with Scripture. Moreover, by intending many meanings in speaking the Scripture, God providentially provides believers with the basic material they will need to defend themselves and their faith from error.

Scripture's multifaceted literal sense also enables Thomas and other readers to properly engage prior faithful interpreters of Scripture. This may be more important than it might initially seem. In the case of John 1:1 each of the interpretations of "in the beginning was the Word" is advocated by one or more of the church fathers. If there is only one literal sense of this text, then at least some, and perhaps all, of these interpreters are wrong. As I mentioned above, Thomas is not a credulous bumpkin on this score. If he takes Origen or Augustine or Ambrose or any other prior interpreter of a text to be mistaken either in whole or in part he will say so. Nevertheless, when three interpreters, all of whom are recognized for their wisdom and holiness, advocate distinct interpretations of a text, all of which make true claims that can enhance believers' friendship with God, little is to be gained and much is to be lost in consigning some of them either to error or to the much more slippery and subsidiary terrain of the spiritual sense.

Moreover, a multifaceted literal sense allows Christianity the flexibility it requires as a living tradition, capable of comprehending within its compass a host of interpreters whose manifest wisdom and sanctity of life commend them to us as exemplary interpreters.

Further, for Thomas, theological concerns and the so-called rule of faith regulate scriptural interpretation. Any interpretation that violates the rule of faith as embodied in the creed, for example, could not count as the literal sense. At the same time, then, it would be odd to reject those interpreters whose scriptural interpretations and theological reflections resulted in the creedal formulations that then regulated subsequent interpretation.

The final reason for adopting a multifaceted view of the literal sense of Scripture has to do with what one might call Thomas's theological pedagogy. Thomas's writing is always deeply connected to his teaching. His discussion of Scripture, his commentaries, and his more general theological writing are all designed to deepen his students' love of God. Moreover, at the university level the medieval classroom was not primarily a place where a single voice dispensed data into the pens of docile students. Medieval learning was marked by questioning and disputation. It was a communal affair in ways that we may well have lost. In a brief sentence of his discussion of the multifaceted literal sense in *De potentia* Thomas notes that a multifaceted literal sense of Scripture is in accord with the "dignity of Scripture." This is in part because students and nonacademic believers can draw great delight from the fact that they can find their own best and truest thoughts to be in accord with Scripture. This would lead to further diligent study and in doing this the student would come to love God more. Thus Scripture's dignity is confirmed as it fulfills its end of drawing us into deeper love of God.[15]

These, I suggest, are some of the reasons that Thomas may have for advocating a plurality in the literal sense of Scripture. Because he said so little about this, we cannot be sure about his intentions in this matter. In Thomistic fashion, however, I would claim that these reasons all assert truths to which Thomas would assent and that they do no violence to the context of his remarks.

More importantly, I want to commend the assumptions underlying Thomas's view as those that we too ought to hold. Thus, we should, with Thomas, see Scripture and its interpretation,

15. This reason is offered by Johnson, "Another Look at the Plurality," 139.

not as an end in itself, but as a central way in which God draws us into ever deeper friendship. Further, rather than providing a set of proof texts for doctrine, we should study, interpret, and engage Scripture to deepen and enrich the agreements between Scripture and our doctrine, faith, and practice. In this way we will be able to comprehend all truth, or, in Paul's terms, we will be able to bring every thought captive to Christ.

We should come to learn from and love the exemplary interpreters of Scripture who precede us in the faith. The legitimate diversity in their interpretation of Scripture can both open and regulate diversity in our own interpretation. In this way we can more fully plumb the riches intended by the Holy Spirit in speaking the Scriptures in the first place.

Our study of Scripture both in the seminary classroom and in the congregations and communities where we live and worship should lead us to delight in the discovery of God's truth, especially when that truth deepens our knowledge and love of God and even more when that truth leads us to repent.

To the extent that we share in these Thomistic assumptions about Scripture, God, the world, and ourselves, we must attend to the literal sense of Scripture and hold that the literal sense is multifaceted in the ways that Thomas asserts.

3

Imprisoned or Free?

Text, Status, and Theological Interpretation in the Master/Slave Discourse of Philemon

KEVIN J. VANHOOZER

"When *I* use a word," Humpty Dumpty said, in rather a scornful tone, "it means just what I choose it to mean—neither more nor less."

"The question is," said Alice, "whether you *can* make words mean so many different things."

"The question is," said Humpty Dumpty, "which is to be master—that's all."

Lewis Carroll, *Through the Looking-Glass*

"No one can serve two masters."

Matthew 6:24

The Master/Slave Relation in Philosophical and Theological Hermeneutics

The brief exchange from Lewis Carroll's *Through the Looking-Glass* describes the struggle to control, contain, or channel meaning in terms of a particular relation, namely, that between masters and slaves. Which is to be the master and which the slave: author, text, subject matter, individual interpreter, interpretive community? The hermeneutics of Wonderland appears to be a rather machiavellian affair in which interpretation is ultimately a function of personal preference combined with brute force.

Paul Ricoeur lends impressive philosophical support to Humpty Dumpty's intuition about the creation of meaning: "Reading is, first and foremost, a struggle with the text."[1] The so-called conflict of interpretations pertains not only to readers struggling with texts and authors but also with other readers. This agonistic (Greek *agōn* = "contest") ethos that characterizes the situation in general hermeneutics casts its shadow over a fair amount of biblical interpretation too, where biblical critics struggle with one another in what can often come to resemble a game of methodological one-upmanship. Indeed, according to David Clines, the academy resembles nature, red in tooth and claw, where only the fittest (e.g., most interesting, entertaining, or edifying) interpretations survive.[2]

And what of the church? Where do interpretive power and interpretive authority lie when the church reads Scripture theologically? Robert Morgan notes that interpreters of authoritative texts (e.g., laws, constitutions, scriptures) subordinate themselves to the text or to the author. He calls this the "common-sense view of the privileged status of the text" and associates it with the fact that "we usually want to understand a text because we think the author is worth hearing."[3] In this conversational model of interpretation, we are bound to the author's intention "because the author is alive and has some moral right to be understood as intended."[4] Yet for most texts in the public realm, says Morgan, the moral rights, as well as the "balance of power," shift to the interpreters: "They are the masters or judges of meaning now, for

1. Paul Ricoeur, "World of the Text, World of the Reader," in *A Ricoeur Reader: Reflection and Imagination* (ed. Mario J. Valdés; Toronto: Harvester Wheatsheaf, 1991), 494.
2. David J. A. Clines, "Possibilities and Priorities of Biblical Interpretation in an International Perspective," *Biblical Interpretation* 1 (1993): 67–87.
3. Robert Morgan, *Biblical Interpretation* (Oxford: Oxford University Press, 1988), 6.
4. Ibid.

better or for worse. The interpreters are never mindless servants of the text. . . . They are human agents with their own aims, interests, and rights."[5] The high status of the interpreter implies a lower status for texts: "Texts, like dead men and women, have no rights, no aims, no interests. They can be used in whatever way readers or interpreters choose."[6] On this latter point, at least, Robert Morgan and Humpty Dumpty agree: it is the interpreter who makes the text "useful." Is the theological interpreter thus more like a slave—of the text, its subject matter, its author—or a master, able to pursue his or her own interpretive aims and interests? The problem with this alternative is that no matter how one answers it, somebody or something always suffers; the slave—in Morgan's view, the text—loses freedom: the power of self-determination, the power of free speech.

Humpty Dumpty's forced choice—to be either the slave or master of verbal meaning—brings to mind another philosophical contortionist, Jean-Paul Sartre, who trapped himself inside a similar false dichotomy: "If God exists then the future is determined and I am not free; I am free; therefore, God does not exist." Clearly, Sartre's problem lay in his understanding of the key terms: Who is God? What is freedom? Similar problems attend those who reflect on key terms in theological hermeneutics.

The goal of the present essay is to offer some biblical and dogmatic descriptions of several central notions regularly employed in discussions about theological hermeneutics. Perhaps the most important of these terms is *freedom*. If reading is first and foremost a struggle with the text, as Ricoeur suggests, it only remains to add that the struggle is all about freedom: the freedom to speak, the freedom to interpret, but also the freedom to be heard. What, in particular, is interpretive freedom? May readers say and do just anything with texts, or are there certain constraints on interpreters? If there are constraints on what interpreters may do, what are they, and do they compromise interpretive freedom?

I shall approach such questions obliquely, first, by describing the text as the medium of the author's communicative action—itself a type of freedom—and, second, by means of my own reading

5. Ibid., 6–7.
6. Ibid., 7.

of Philemon. Proceeding in this way allows me both to stake out my position and to demonstrate it by my interpretive practice, something conspicuously absent in my previous forays into the thickets of theological hermeneutics. Why Philemon? Because the master/slave discourse in this brief Pauline epistle serves not only as a case study for biblical interpretation but also as a metaphor for the central problem of theological hermeneutics inasmuch as it bears on the question of the relative status of author and interpreter (and interpretive community).[7]

What Philemon provides is not a rule or principle for interpretation so much as a *paradigm* for the theological interpretation of Scripture.[8] Specifically, Philemon offers a normative display of how a reader with theological understanding ought to respond to apostolic discourse. As such, it affords us an intriguing glimpse into the question of how we, also, ought to respond to apostolic discourse. I therefore propose to read Philemon as a treatise on the ethics of theological interpretation. *Status* is the operative category for this proposal, and one whose importance has not been sufficiently acknowledged in previous discussions, for to determine the relative status of text and reader is to discern where interpretive authority, power, and freedom really lie.

The great lesson of twentieth-century hermeneutics is that understanding is a matter not strictly of epistemology but, more fundamentally, of ontology: human being. Thus the distinctiveness of theological hermeneutics will be a function of the distinctiveness of Christian anthropology.[9] After all, no status question

7. It also bears on the related question of the authoritative status of the biblical text, as George Lindbeck rightly notes: "It seems that disagreements over interpretive modes even more than over doctrinal content are at the heart of the present crisis of biblical authority"; "Postcritical Canonical Interpretation: Three Modes of Retrieval," in *Theological Exegesis: Essays in Honor of Brevard S. Childs* (ed. Christopher Seitz and Kathryn Greene-McCreight; Grand Rapids: Eerdmans, 1999), 40.

8. A paradigm is a story with a character who models exemplary conduct. Richard Hays's book is concerned with how ethicists appeal to Scripture. His typology distinguishes between rules, principles, paradigms, and symbolic worlds; *The Moral Vision of the New Testament: A Contemporary Introduction to New Testament Ethics* (San Francisco: Harper, 1996), 209. In the case of Philemon, as we shall see, it is the *implied* reader (the implied Philemon!) whose response is paradigmatic.

9. For further development of this point, see Kevin J. Vanhoozer, "Discourse on Matter: Hermeneutics and the 'Miracle' of Understanding," *International Journal of Systematic Theology* 7 (2005): 5–37.

is more fundamental than Kant's query, "What is man?" Here, a reading of Philemon proves instructive in terms of what Richard Hays calls "symbolic world"—one way that ethicists derive moral norms from Scripture. By "symbolic world" Hays calls attention to the storied categories or narrative representations of the human condition: narrated depictions of the character of God through which Christians interpret reality.[10] Perhaps the most important of these categories is the notion that the world itself is being renewed "in Christ." As we shall see, being "in Christ" becomes the overarching theological and anthropological category through which Christians interpret their own status vis-à-vis God, God's word, and other human interpreters.

Modern and postmodern interpreters are more inclined to assume a status posture of mastery toward texts than to confess themselves slaves, not least because they view freedom in terms of the "power-to-do" and the "power-to-choose."[11] Historical critics, for example, strive to master the text in the sense of explaining the process of its composition and judging the merits of its factual claims. Meanwhile, ideology critics are busy securing their textual manumission by exposing, then deconstructing, the various devices by which texts seek to constrain their interpretive freedom. Such critics successfully "free" themselves from any need to respond personally to what is said in the text. Perhaps they employ a variation of Sartre's maxim: "If God has spoken then the meaning of life is determinate and I am not free to make my own meaning; I do make my own meaning, therefore God has not spoken."

No philosopher makes more of the master/slave relation than Hegel, for whom it serves as centerpiece of his magnum opus, *The Phenomenology of Mind*. From Philemon to phenomenology—who would have thought? The master/slave relationship is for Hegel a parable of how consciousness—self-understanding—emerges and, as such, is central to his whole philosophical system. Accordingly, he makes a fitting conversation partner as we assess two kinds of hermeneutical wisdom (i.e., the philosophical and theological).

10. Hays, *Moral Vision of the New Testament*, 209.
11. See Paul Ricoeur, *Freedom and Nature: The Voluntary and the Involuntary* (Evanston, IL: Northwestern University Press, 1966).

What we have in Hegel is a philosophical account of human being, understanding, and freedom—in effect, an essay on the interpreter's *ontological* status. Contra Descartes's declaration of ontological independence—"I think, therefore I am"—Hegel believes that self-consciousness exists only to the extent that it is acknowledged by another. Because we cannot bear to be thought of as "objects" by others, however, we struggle to subject "others" to *our* consciousness. So we objectify, and thereby enslave, the other. This is a self-defeating strategy, however, because what we want as individuals is recognition, and we do not get the recognition we desire from things. Master and slave are thus caught up in a life-and-death struggle for recognition (status), a "dialectical" struggle marked by a logical reversal in which the master, becoming increasingly dependent on the slave, and the slave, becoming increasingly independent by proving "useful" to the master, switch roles.[12] The key element in this master/slave dialectic is a hidden and necessary reciprocity: the identity of each is dependent on the other.[13]

A similar dialectic complicates the relations of author, text, and reader.[14] Just as Hegel argues that the other's acknowledgment not only recognizes but *constitutes* me as a subject, so a prominent trend in contemporary philosophical hermeneutics is to say that textual meaning is not only recognized but *constituted* by interpreters. Just as the master's identity is dependent upon the slave, so the author's or text's identity is dependent upon the reader; here, too, the hermeneutical polarities are reversed, along with the status of the respective parties to interpretation.

12. "Each is therefore the inverse of what it immediately and superficially is given as being"; J. N. Findlay, in *Hegel's Phenomenology of Spirit* (Oxford: Oxford University Press, 1997), 522.

13. The master/slave dialectic plays an important role in Hegel's account of the necessary dialectical process through which *Geist* comes to self-consciousness, a process within which Hegel locates even the God-world distinction/relationship. The Christian theologian will be right to demur at the point where Hegel (or his successors) attempts to paint the God-world relation by the same metaphysical numbers. The question is whether a panentheistic view of the God-world relation can preserve the Creator-creation distinction and hence God's authoritative status as "the Father almighty, Maker of heaven and earth."

14. For the material in this paragraph, I am indebted to Bruce Benson's unpublished response ("Lordship, Bondage, and the Unhappy Interpreter") to an earlier draft of my essay.

On the one hand, authors appear to be masters of their discourse, lording the text over the reader. In one sense, then, we can speak of the "reading contained or implied in the text." Such a picture has little scope for interpretive freedom, however, and gives rise to what Ricoeur describes as "readers terrorized by the decree of predestination striking their reading."[15] On the other hand, without the reader, there is no configuring act at work in the text, no world unfolded before the text, so much so that the merely historicizing question—what did the text say?—"remains under the control of the properly hermeneutical question—what does the text say to me and what do I say to the text?"[16] Again we see how texts and readers are caught up in a paradox of freedom and constraint that would seem to entail not hierarchy but mutual (i.e., dialectical) reciprocity.

To this point we have been discussing the status of authors, texts, and readers in general. The issue of interpretive freedom and constraint becomes even more acute as we turn to consider the theological interpretation of Scripture. Interpreters who value their freedom may be reluctant to inhabit a symbolic world in which divine infinite freedom and authority appears to overpower human finite freedom. This, at least, is how Sartre's problem is transposed to the domain of theological hermeneutics. According to Nietzsche, for example, "God" is the ultimate constraint on interpretive creativity, which is why he insisted that "there are no facts, only interpretations." Nietzsche views the master/slave relation as a metaphor for two contrasting modes of morality. The slave morality he associates with Christianity is servile, fearful, and ultimately a denial of the creative life force. Creative interpretation is for him the royal road to human (or should I say, *übermenschlich*) flourishing. Unfortunately, Nietzsche was never able to get beyond this dichotomy, with its concomitant view of unconstrained human freedom. The result: a hermeneutic of the unconstrained will to power in which the birth of the (creative) reader requires the death of the (constraining) author (human and/or divine).

So much for the backdrop. The present essay has two main parts and a conclusion. I begin by sketching the contours (and

15. Paul Ricoeur, "Between the Text and Its Readers," in *A Ricoeur Reader: Reflection and Imagination* (ed. Mario J. Valdés; Toronto: Harvester Wheatsheaf, 1991), 398.
16. Ibid., 409.

certain in-flight corrections) of my own interpretation theory and by saying what is theological about it. The second part illustrates how the approach works by interpreting Philemon. The two parts of the essay are mutually reinforcing because, as I have already intimated, the *matter* of Philemon speaks directly to the *method* of interpretation I here commend. Paul's letter is a practical treatise on theological hermeneutics, broadly conceived, inasmuch as it illustrates *what is involved in understanding the apostolic discourse about our new reality "in Christ."* Moreover, Paul's epistle gives us a clear picture as to how Paul intended and expected his discourse to be understood. Finally, as is well known, Philemon speaks to the master/slave relation, which in turn serves as my metaphorical way into questions concerning the relative standing (status) of author, text, subject matter, and community of readers. Philemon is useful to the contemporary church as a model of how Christian readers exemplify both freedom and restraint in their theological interpretation of the Bible.

Theological Hermeneutics: From Divine Discourse to Theodrama

All texts have contexts, and my books are no exception. In my earlier work in hermeneutics, I was preoccupied with answering some of the more radical exponents of postmodernity whose work was being appropriated by increasing numbers of biblical scholars and theologians in the 1990s. The epitome of this *fin de siècle* deconstructive frenzy was *The Postmodern Bible*, a text produced not by an author but by a collective, and motivated not by the hermeneutics of suspicion but by the suspicion of hermeneutics according to which interpretations, and methods of interpretation themselves, far from being natural or necessary, are in fact arbitrary sociopolitical constructions and thus so many ideological expressions of the will to power.[17]

17. Elizabeth A. Castelli, Stephen D. Moore, Gary A. Phillips, and Regina M. Schwartz, eds., *The Postmodern Bible* (New Haven: Yale University Press, 1995).

This, at least, is what the hermeneutical landscape looked like to me from the vantage point of my academic hilltop.[18] So I raced down the hill and ran into the global village and warned, like Nietzsche's Madman, of the deaths of God and author alike. My concern to preserve authorial rights had less to do with establishing a principle of authority, however, than it did with providing readers with a pathway to *transcendence*, that is, with some means of getting beyond themselves and their own thoughts.[19] Many villagers were nevertheless puzzled by what appeared to them to be my hermeneutical hysteria. I quickly came to identify with Nietzsche's Madman: "I have come too early, this tremendous event is still on its way."

In any case, I formulated what I would now call a theological general hermeneutic that sought to restore certain authorial rights, especially the right to be heard.[20] It was a theological *general* hermeneutic because I argued that readers have a mandate to do justice to the authors not only of the Bible but also of *all* texts. "Doing justice" in this context is not a matter of recovering the psychological intentions an author may have had (the textual evidence for what an author "planned" to say is neither adequate nor available) but rather of describing what an author *did* say/do by using certain words in a certain fashion.[21] I saw this mandate

18. Throughout the 1990s when I was teaching theology at the University of Edinburgh, I was also involved in a course on contemporary literary theory for M.A. students in the comparative literature program. My own role was limited to leading seminars on Paul Ricoeur for a couple of weeks, but by that time many of the students had already decided that there were no norms in interpretation beyond what feels (i.e., reads) good to me.

19. To some extent, all good interpretation issues in a moment of transcendence. Such "transcendence" is not necessarily theological in the strict sense of pertaining to God, though that is the ultimate aim of my theological interpretation of Scripture.

20. See especially Kevin J. Vanhoozer, *Is There a Meaning in This Text? The Bible, the Reader, and the Morality of Literary Knowledge* (Grand Rapids: Zondervan, 1998).

21. In this respect, doing justice to authors and their communicative action is similar to doing justice to human agents in general, especially when their actions may be praiseworthy or blameworthy or liable to some kind of sanction as in a court of law—hence the subtitle of my book: "The *Morality* of Literary Knowledge." If, as I there argued, the meaning of a text is simply what the author said/did, then it is incumbent on the interpreter to ascribe only those communicative actions to the author that the author enacted. Of course, as in

as entailed by the Golden Rule and by the ninth commandment: we should treat the text of others as we would have others treat our texts, and we must not bear false witness to what authors have said and done in their texts. It was a *theological* general hermeneutic because I construed the postmodern dissolution of determinate meaning as the result of certain theological moves, in particular, a denial of orthodox Christian doctrines such as creation, incarnation, and sanctification. Building on George Steiner's insight that "God" somehow underwrites language and interpretation, I adopted an Augustinian ("I believe in order to understand") approach in response and argued that Christian belief—trinitarian theology, to be precise—was the necessary condition for textual understanding.[22]

I have since come to see, thanks to my critics (their name is Legion!), that my argument did not attend sufficiently to what is distinctive about the Bible or to its interpretation in the church.[23] Consequently, I am now inclined to pursue a theological *special* hermeneutic that recognizes (contra Jowett) the ways in which the Bible is *not* to be read "like any other book."[24] What has remained constant, however, are my convictions (1) that dealing with texts is ultimately a mode of engaging persons and with what persons have done by means of writing;[25] (2) that as biblical interpreters, we are ultimately dealing with the Holy Spirit speaking and presenting Jesus Christ in the Scriptures; and (3) that as biblical interpreters, our task is to discern what

a court of law, we may never have 100 percent certainty as to an agent's intentions, but all that is required is proof beyond a reasonable doubt, and this is usually available.

22. For further development of these controversial points, see Vanhoozer, *Is There a Meaning in This Text?* 456–57. The basic premise of my argument is that the paradigm of communicative agency is the Triune God. For Steiner's view, see his *Real Presences* (Chicago: University of Chicago Press, 1989).

23. An important bridge piece may be found in Kevin J. Vanhoozer, *First Theology: God, Scripture, and Hermeneutics* (Downers Grove, IL: InterVarsity, 2002), chap. 6: "From Speech Acts to Scripture Acts: The Covenant of Discourse and the Discourse of the Covenant."

24. See Benjamin Jowett, "On the Interpretation of Scripture" (1860) in his *The Interpretation of Scripture and Other Essays* (London: Routledge, 1907).

25. Cf. Nicholas Wolterstorff, who articulates this conviction as well as anyone in his "A Response to Trevor Hart," in *Renewing Biblical Interpretation* (ed. Craig Bartholomew, Colin Greene, and Karl Möller; Grand Rapids: Zondervan, 2000), 335–41.

the Spirit is saying by means of what the human authors of Scripture have said.[26] What has changed is the way I understand this divine discourse, its relation to Scripture, and the form that our understanding must take. The change is not a conversion, however, much less a retraction of my former position, but rather its enrichment.

Scripture and Divine Discourse

Theories of interpretation must do more than describe what readers do, even when these readers make up the community of saints. The church is not an error-free zone; false teaching, fallenness, and corporate pride all conspire to subvert the good news. There is a constant temptation to rewrite those parts of Scripture that sound most dissonant to our culture. Given the inevitable conflict of biblical interpretations, where does authority lie? Whose say-so counts, and why? My own *Is There a Meaning in This Text?* offers a normative account to these questions: at the very minimum, interpreters *ought* to read in order to grasp what the author has said and done. Though other interpretive interests are legitimate, I argue that to go wrong here—in describing what authors were saying/doing—is to miss the very raison d'être of the text. My earlier focus was thus squarely on authorial discourse in contrast to those whose primary focus was on the final form of the text as a witness to Christ or on the church as an interpretive community.[27] The christological subject matter and the ecclesial community figure prominently in my approach, to be sure, but not independently of authorial discourse.

The Norm: Divine Discourse

Theories are most susceptible to deconstruction if it can be shown that they depend on certain key decisions that could have been otherwise. So: why *discourse*? and *whose* discourse? The

26. I agree with Wolterstorff ("Response to Trevor Hart," 339–40) that there is a difference between understanding *why* someone says something (a question for historians and psychologists) and *what* a person said—his or her speech act. The latter is the question for hermeneutics as "the art of discerning the discourse in the work" (Ricoeur).

27. See Lindbeck, "Postcritical Canonical Interpretation."

short answer, to both questions, is that theological interpretation of Scripture is a matter of reading the Bible to hear the word of God. To be sure, there are a number of subsidiary aims that interpreters can have: to discover something about a particular language (e.g., Greek) at the time of the text's composition; to reconstruct the history of a text's composition; to describe the text's employment of rhetorical strategies; to study the material conditions—social, economic, gender—of a text's production; to learn more about a subject matter by joining a text-generated conversation; to learn more about oneself in light of the mode of being displayed in the text; even to imagine what a text would have meant had *I* been its author.

These interests give rise to interpretive theories that contribute many legitimate and interesting insights. To approach the Bible with a theological interest, however, is to read in order to hear what God is saying to the church—to discern the *divine* discourse in the *canonical* work.[28] Readers ideally should approach the text in a manner that corresponds to what it is. Everything thus depends on how we understand the nature or ontology of the biblical text. What exactly are we reading? The answer, I believe, is that the biblical text is the divinely authorized and commissioned human witness to God's work of creation and redemption, especially as these culminate in the person and work of Jesus Christ and, as such, that the Bible itself is a form of the word of God. While a full discussion of this identification is beyond the scope of the present essay, let me indicate three lines of argumentation in favor of identifying Scripture with God's word written.

Scriptural Testimony. The Bible portrays God as a speech agent (e.g., Exod. 3; Matt. 3:17) and prophets as divinely commissioned speech agents who speak for God (e.g., "The word of the Lord that came to Hosea" [Hos. 1:1]). In addition, there are also reports of human authors writing down words that God told them to write, especially in relation to the covenant (Exod. 24:4; 34:27; Josh. 24:26; Jer. 30:2). Furthermore, the New Testament frequently cites the Old Testament in ways that suggest that it is divine speech.

---

28. The superiority of a theological interpretive interest follows from the theological interest of the biblical texts themselves. Werner Jeanrond argues that one's choice of "reading genre" must be appropriate to the text genre in order to do justice to the text; *Text and Interpretation as Categories of Theological Thinking* (New York: Crossroad, 1988), 120.

For example, Matthew 1:22 cites Isaiah 7:14 as "what the Lord had spoken by the prophet," and Acts 1:16 records Peter referring to words of Scripture as that which "the Holy Spirit spoke beforehand by the mouth of David." Peter later speaks of "what God foretold by the mouth of all the prophets, that his Christ should suffer" (Acts 3:18). The link between "what Scripture says" and "what God says" is such that Paul can on occasion substitute the one for the other (see Gal. 3:8; Rom. 9:17).

Two other, more programmatic, statements cover the Old Testament as a whole: "All Scripture is *theopneustos*": inspired (not inspiring), "God breathed" (2 Tim. 3:16); "Men moved by the Holy Spirit [*pneumatos hagiou*] spoke from God" (2 Pet. 1:21). There is also evidence that the New Testament writers considered their own writings as similarly commissioned, though this time from the risen Lord (1 Cor. 14:37; 1 Thess. 2:13; cf. 2 Pet. 3:15–16).[29] There is ample testimony, then, that *biblical discourse is both what humans have said through the Spirit and what God has said through humans*.

Church Tradition. From the apostolic age onward, the church has always recognized certain writings that carried divine authority and served as a divine rule for faith and life, hence the phrase *Holy Scriptures*. Though there was (and is) some dispute as to which books should be counted as Scripture, the threefold basis for recognizing a text as the word of God has by and large remained constant: (1) its divine authorization and commissioning (e.g., of prophets and apostles); (2) its Christ-centered gospel content: Christ is the Word to whom Scripture bears authorized witness; and (3) its spiritual fruitfulness and didactic profitability for training in righteousness as continuously acknowledged and experienced in the church catholic.[30]

There is a striking unanimity in the testimony of the church fathers with regard to Scripture as the word of God: "*All* the

29. For further development of this line of argumentation, see Benjamin B. Warfield, *The Inspiration and Authority of the Bible* (Philipsburg, NJ: Presbyterian & Reformed, 1979); and Herman Bavinck, *Reformed Dogmatics*, vol. 1: *Prolegomena* (ed. John Bolt; trans. John Vriend; Grand Rapids: Baker, 2003), chap. 13: "The Inspiration of Scripture."

30. I have taken, and slightly revised, these three points from J. I. Packer, "Scripture," in *New Dictionary of Theology* (ed. Sinclair B. Ferguson and David F. Wright; Downers Grove, IL: InterVarsity, 1988), 628.

Church Fathers, without exception, believed that the Bible was God's word written."[31] For example, in his *First Epistle to the Corinthians*, Clement of Rome speaks of "the Holy Scriptures which are true and inspired by the Holy Spirit" (45.2). Though Clement has primarily the Old Testament in mind, he also states that the apostle Paul had written to the Corinthians "under inspiration of the Spirit" (47.3). Athenagoras goes so far as to liken the Spirit to a flutist who uses the human authors as his instruments (*Plea for the Christians* 7). Augustine, however, speaks of the human authors of Scripture not as mere instruments but as disciples, and he says that the aim of Scripture's readers "is simply to find out the thoughts and wishes of those by whom it was written down, and through them the will of God, which we believe these men followed as they spoke" (*On Christian Doctrine* 2.9). The final representative word belongs to Hippolytus: "There is, brethren, one God, the knowledge of whom we gain from the Holy Scriptures, and from no other source. . . . All of us who wish to practice piety will be unable to learn its practice from any other quarter than the oracles of God. Whatever things, then, the Holy Scriptures declare, at these let us look, and whatever they teach, that let us learn" (*Homily on the Heresy of Noestus* 9).

Liturgical Practice. In many churches, the reading of Scripture concludes with a phrase of recognition: "The word of the Lord."

Now that we see why the church views the Bible as God's word in written form, we need to inquire further into the nature and function of words. The most important development in twentieth-century philosophy of language was the turn from the semiotics of *langue* (language as detached element in a signifying system)

31. Gerald Bray, "The Church Fathers and Their Use of Scripture," in *The Trustworthiness of God: Perspectives on the Nature of Scripture* (ed. Paul Helm and Carl R. Trueman; Grand Rapids: Eerdmans, 2002), 159. Cf. J. N. D. Kelly: "It goes without saying that the fathers envisaged the whole of the Bible as inspired"; *Early Christian Doctrines* (rev. ed.; San Francisco: Harper & Row, 1978), 61. Christopher A. Hall reaches a similar conclusion after surveying four representative church fathers from the West and four from the East: "All agreed that the Bible is an inspired text"; *Reading Scripture with the Church Fathers* (Downers Grove, IL: InterVarsity, 1998), 132. Finally, though he grounds the authority of Scripture in its divine origin (*Institutes of the Christian Religion* 1.7.1), Calvin too is impressed by the unvarying testimony of the church to Scripture as God's word (1.8.12).

to the hermeneutics of *parole* (language as concrete instance of contextualized speech) and the concomitant emphasis on the importance of word *use* in determining meaning. The discovery that authors not only signify or communicate—in the narrow sense of conveying information—but *do* various things in, with, and through their words (e.g., promise, command, warn, encourage, affirm, deny) opens up rich new possibilities for thinking about the Bible as God's word written. Most importantly, it allows us to view interpretation in terms of personal engagement and not merely information processing. It follows that interpretation is a kind of "status transaction" that involves, among other things, recognizing what speech acts "belong" to which persons and of ascribing certain "standings" to persons in light of the speech acts that those persons perform.[32] For example, one who says "I saw an empty tomb" acquires the normative standing of a witness, a standing that alters the relation between speaker and hearer: "Asserting that so-and-so introduces into human relationships the (prima facie) right to be taken at one's word that so-and-so."[33]

Let us define discourse, then, as "what someone says to someone in some way about something." As we have just seen, saying is a kind of doing—hence the term *speech act*. There are three aspects or dimensions to a speech act: locution (the saying), illocution (what is done *in* saying something), and perlocution (what is done *by* saying something). Hermeneutics is "the art of discerning the discourse in the work."[34] If the words of writers in the Bible are themselves bearers of divine discourse, then theological interpretation of Scripture is "the art of discerning the divine discourse in the work." The Bible is a medium of divine illocutionary and perlocutionary action, a creaturely reality that has been set aside—sanctified—for a divine purpose.[35]

32. Here I am following Wolterstorff's analysis of speaking as a way of acquiring rights and responsibilities or what he calls "normative standing" (viz., status); *Divine Discourse: Philosophical Reflections on the Claim That God Speaks* (Cambridge: Cambridge University Press, 1995), 83–85.

33. Ibid., 85.

34. Paul Ricoeur, *Hermeneutics and the Human Sciences* (Cambridge: Cambridge University Press, 1981), 138.

35. For a fuller explanation of this point, see John Webster, *Holy Scripture: A Dogmatic Sketch* (Cambridge: Cambridge University Press, 2004).

To be precise: the Bible is a dual-authored, human and divine discourse, the means by which someone (ultimately the Spirit) says something (ultimately Jesus Christ) to someone (ultimately the church) in certain ways (viz., literary forms).

Theological Interpretation: Understanding Divine Authorial Discourse

Theological hermeneutics, we have said, is the art of discerning the divine discourse in the work. The work in question, of course, is the Christian Scriptures. The concept of "work" implies something about the wholeness or unity of a discourse, and the term of choice that describes the unity of God's word written, at least on a formal level, is "canon." Premodern interpreters had no trouble reading Scripture as a canonical whole. They were adept at understanding one part of Scripture in light of other parts, whether the parts in question were single verses or whole testaments. Such is not the case with modern interpreters who, alert to the humanity of the biblical texts—the historically and culturally conditioned nature of their composition—are more likely to highlight diversity and differences. If theological hermeneutics is a matter of discerning the unified divine discourse in the work, however, it becomes incumbent on the interpreter to give an account of the kind of theological wholeness we may ascribe to and discern in these texts.

What justifies the practice of interpreting one part of Scripture by reference to other parts? Three recent accounts of reading the Bible as a unified whole make appeal to factors other than authorial discourse. The short-lived *biblical theology* movement of the mid-twentieth century believed that the Scriptures were united by a shared theology and by common concepts. The *biblical narrative* approach that followed in the 1970s suggested that the books comprising the canon are connected by the recital of God's mighty acts and by the rendering of the identity of God and Jesus Christ. More recently, the focus of those who appeal to biblical narrative has turned to its function in projecting a symbolic world that shapes ecclesial identity and provides an all-embracing interpretive framework that the church imaginatively inhabits. Finally, the *biblical canon* approach discerns unity in the way in which the final form of the Scriptures is so textually and intertextually shaped as to function as a witness to Jesus Christ, to what God did in and through his servant/Son (first Israel and then definitively Jesus Christ) for the people of God.[36]

No one of these three approaches by itself adequately accounts for the practice of reading Scripture as a unified whole. While each calls our attention to a certain mode of canonical unity, not every book in the canon exhibits the unity proposed by any single mode.[37] Lindbeck worries that his own narrated symbolic-world approach—in which meaning is a function of embodying the universe rendered by the text in particular social settings—leaves the actual use of the text in shaping life and thought unspecified. Furthermore, given the diversity of narrated textual worlds in the New Testament (i.e., the four Gospels), the prospect of synthesizing their ethical and theological perspectives is hardly self-evident: "Without a synthesis, however, it becomes impossible to appeal to Scripture as a whole for the contemporary guidance of the church."[38] According to Lindbeck, there can be any number of "skillful" performances that use the text in a coherent fashion; the problem lies in discerning whose sense of wholeness most faithfully expresses the truth of the gospel: "But it is the chaos of opinion on how to answer precisely that question that is at the heart of the contemporary crisis of biblical authority."[39] The church needs some way of determining whose performance of the canonical whole corresponds to the truth of the gospel.

Lindbeck himself is now of the opinion that the way out of the crisis may be authorial discourse interpretation, the

36. My description of these three approaches to theological interpretation conflates (and revises) two other accounts of the contemporary situation: Lindbeck ("Postcritical Canonical Interpretation") and Nicholas Wolterstorff ("The Unity behind the Canon," in *One Scripture or Many? Canon from Biblical, Theological, and Philosophical Perspectives* [ed. Christine Helmer and Christof Landmesser; Oxford: Oxford University Press, 2004], 221). Interestingly, the influence of Karl Barth may be seen in all three approaches, though to develop this point is beyond the scope of the present essay.

37. So Wolterstorff, "Unity behind the Canon," 222.

38. Lindbeck, "Postcritical Canonical Interpretation," 39. I am here reminded of Robert Davidson's comment during a committee meeting for the Church of Scotland on the topic of biblical hermeneutics and human sexuality: "There isn't such a thing as *the* biblical view on anything, not even God."

39. Lindbeck, "Postcritical Canonical Interpretation," 44.

only nonarbitrary criterion for choosing between alternative construals of canonical wholeness. Nicholas Wolterstorff, Lindbeck's representative of the "canonical interpretation for authorial discourse" approach, points out that there is no such thing as "the sense of the text" in the abstract; there is only what this or that person means by using the words and sentences in discourse.[40] Lindbeck's own example of such performance interpretation is telling: "Instead of reading Swift's *Modest Proposal* as satire, one might take it as a serious recommendation to cannibalize Irish infants."[41] Decisions about what a text means depend on *whose performance*—whose discourse—it is. This thought exposes the weakness of Brevard Childs's notion of "canonical intention." *Whose* intention—whose discourse, whose performance, whose illocutionary action—is it? What makes just this moment in the historical process of canonical formation—just these texts in just this, their final, form—the theologically authoritative witness to Jesus Christ? Though Childs himself does not say so, his claim that the canon is a unified authoritative witness to Jesus Christ "is formally equivalent to believing that the Bible is so inspired as to be ultimately the work of a single Author."[42]

What makes something a unified work? The present essay is a single work, even though it cites sentences from the works of other authors, because I chose what to include and how to arrange the elements and judged the piece to have satisfied my demand for completeness (wholeness): "To authorize a sequence of words *as a work* is to declare that one wants one's readers to read it as a totality, on the ground that only thus will they experience the kind of completeness . . . that one was aiming at."[43] To read the canon as a unified discourse, then, is to assume that one is authorized to read its constituent parts as a totality. The only justification of this latter assumption is something "outside" the text itself that is the ground of the latter's coherence: the presence or absence of a certain

40. See Wolterstorff, *Divine Discourse*, chap. 10: "Performance Interpretation."
41. Lindbeck, "Postcritical Canonical Interpretation," 40.
42. Paul R. Noble, *The Canonical Approach: A Critical Reconstruction of the Hermeneutics of Brevard S. Childs* (Leiden: Brill, 1995), 333.
43. Wolterstorff, "Unity behind the Canon," 226.

intentional action, namely, someone authorizing the text as a work.[44]

Interpreting Scripture as a divine work—a unified discourse made up of diverse human discourses—along the lines that Wolterstorff suggests has the additional advantage, as Lindbeck recognizes, of retrieving patterns of premodern theological interpretation.[45] As Clement of Alexandria puts it: "The entire Scripture is one book and was spoken by one Holy Spirit" (*Commentary on Isaiah* 29.11–12).[46] Augustine agrees, saying that in all the things spoken in Scripture there is "one discourse" (*unus sermo*) and that out of the many mouths of the human authors comes "one word" (*unum verbum*) (*Exposition of Psalm* 103.4.1).

To do full justice to this insight concerning "the one and the many" of biblical discourse requires us to recognize the Bible as a stratified semantic reality. On one stratum exists the historical discourse of the diverse human authors. This stratum has an intelligibility and integrity of its own. To the extent that God commissions and appropriates prophetic and apostolic testimony, this level should also be considered God's word. However, this stratum alone does not exhaust what the historic Christian tradition typically means when it confesses the Bible to be God's word, for another stratum of divine discourse emerges at a higher, canonical, level of complexity.[47] What God is doing at this level *depends* on the human discourse, but it cannot be reduced to

44. Ibid., 228. Wolterstorff leaves open the possibility that the Bible as God's word may be seen either as one single work or as sixty-six individual works, God's collected works. Below I argue for the former option on the basis of the nature and function of Scripture's subject matter.

45. Lindbeck, "Postcritical Canonical Interpretation," 50.

46. Cited in Robert Louis Wilken, *The Spirit of Early Christian Thought* (New Haven: Yale University Press, 2003), 62.

47. The phenomenon of "emergence" in the natural sciences is somewhat analogous. For example, biological phenomena are dependent on physical phenomena but cannot be reduced to the physical level. Rather, when physical things reach a certain level of complexity, properly biological phenomena emerge and require the distinct concepts and principles of biology to account for them. For a defense of the notion of stratified reality, see Alister E. McGrath, *A Scientific Theology*, vol. 2: *Reality* (Grand Rapids: Eerdmans, 2002), chap. 10: "Critical Realism: Engaging with a Stratified Reality." For an account of how "mind" emerges from "matter," see Philip Clayton, *Mind and Emergence: From Quantum to Consciousness* (Oxford: Oxford University Press, 2004). As far as I know, I am the first to apply concepts such as emergence and supervenience to biblical

human discourse.[48] When read in light of the canonical whole and its center, Jesus Christ, we begin to see what the divine author is doing in, with, and through the various biblical parts. This is especially important in explaining how nonprophetic texts—texts whose authors are not explicit spokesmen or spokeswomen for God—can nevertheless be counted as divine discourse. I believe that this theory of divine authorial discourse has the dual merit of accounting for traditional modes of theological interpretation of Scripture and of doing so in a way that takes full advantage of contemporary developments in philosophy of language, especially the notion of illocutionary acts.[49]

Interpretation is all about discerning illocutions and recognizing what an author is doing with his or her words. Authors can, of course, do several things at once at different levels. One way of construing the literal sense would be in terms of what an author is *primarily* or perhaps most *obviously* doing. To know what an author is doing, however, one needs to discern the genre of his or her text act: Is she writing history or fiction? Is she being serious or ironic? prophetic or apocalyptic? Interpreters can determine what the author is doing with each sentential part only by considering it in light of the higher level of the literary whole. Because God is the ultimate author of the whole of Scripture, however, some

interpretation. See also Vanhoozer, *Is There a Meaning in This Text?* 265, 328–31; and idem, *First Theology*, 191–94.

48. The technical term for this relation is supervenience and has been used to describe the way in which human thoughts *depend* on brain states but cannot be *reduced* to brain states. I am developing the notion of the stratification of God's word somewhat differently from McGrath, for whom the biblical texts are only one level among the various strata of revelation that include patterns of worship, institutional structures, religious experience, and church tradition. All these are levels in the "crater" of revelation caused by the "revelational explosion" of the history of Jesus; *A Scientific Theology*, vol. 3: *Theory* (Grand Rapids: Eerdmans, 2003), 144–49.

49. J. L. Austin was the first to use the term *illocution* in his *How to Do Things with Words* (Oxford: Oxford University Press, 1962). John Searle systematized the notion in his *Speech Acts: An Essay in the Philosophy of Language* (Cambridge: Cambridge University Press, 1969). See also William Alston, *Philosophy of Language* (Englewood Cliffs, NJ: Prentice Hall, 1964); and idem, *Illocutionary Acts and Sentence Meaning* (Ithaca, NY: Cornell University Press, 2000). For a survey and constructive proposal concerning the role of illocutions in biblical hermeneutics, see Richard S. Briggs, *Words in Action: Speech Act Theory and Biblical Interpretation* (Edinburgh: T&T Clark, 2001).

illocutions will emerge only in light of the canonical context: the whole of Scripture considered as a single work. It is primarily at the canonical level that we see what the divine author is doing in, with, and through the various interrelated parts of Scripture.

To miss what God is saying and doing at various levels of the biblical text is to risk interpreting in ways that yield "thin" interpretations only. In contrast, theological interpretations offer "thick descriptions" of the divine discourse in the work that, in addition to attending to the specific things that God is saying and doing at the level of a particular sentence, consistently relate the parts to the canonical work as a whole and so discern other illocutionary levels where God is doing things like "administering the covenant" or "presenting Christ." Reading for divine authorial discourse consequently yields what we might call a "deflationary" account of the older distinction between literal and figurative senses. Rather than attempting to draw a hard and fast distinction between the historical and the allegorical sense, the theological interpreter of Scripture would do better simply to describe the various things that authors (including the divine author) are doing in their texts at different levels, including the canonical. Theological interpretation is not a matter of breaking some code ("this means that") but of grasping everything that God is doing in and with the various strata of biblical discourse.

In sum: theological interpretation is the process of discerning the discourse, human and divine, in the canonical work. Whose discourse counts? I answer: that of the original historical author and the divine author who commissions, enables, authorizes, and accompanies it. It is not redundant to specify the divinely appropriated or commissioned discourse as the historical author's. Certain postmodern interpreters are happy to assume a quasi-authorial role; they do so each time they become the first to ascribe a certain meaning to the text. As Lindbeck notes, however, even those who reject authorial discourse in theory cannot escape it in practice: "Fear of the intentional fallacy, it seems, prevents them from recognizing that their exegetical practice is (fortunately) full of appeals to authorial intention."[50] Understanding,

50. Lindbeck, "Postcritical Canonical Interpretation," 48. Lindbeck is careful to distinguish *intending to* (planning to do something) from *intentional action* (actually doing something, enacting).

narrowly conceived, is a matter of recognizing what illocutionary acts an author has performed and is performing.

In a broader sense, however, understanding discourse goes beyond merely recognizing illocutions and includes right reception and right response. Such rightness is not a product of hermeneutic will power but of the Spirit's work in the reader. Those who read "in the Spirit" lay themselves open to the effects of the text and are thus transformed by the renewing of their minds (Rom. 12:2). As the church fathers well knew, biblical interpretation both requires and results in spiritual formation: "The dialectic between spiritual growth, character formation and understanding Scripture is a crucial patristic insight."[51] And it is a crucial Reformation insight to insist that God speaks in *and through* Scripture. The phrase *and through* calls attention to the role of perlocution (*per* + *locutus* = "through speaking"): what authors aim to effect by speaking. The author of the Fourth Gospel, for example, explicitly says that he intends his narrative (the illocutionary act of displaying the life of Jesus) to *persuade* his readers to believe in Jesus Christ (John 20:31).

I agree with Karl Barth that the Spirit is the "subjective reality of revelation" and with William Alston that perlocutions supervene on illocutions.[52] The Spirit's work in illumining readers and effecting perlocutions builds on the meaning and force of what is said in the text. In Calvin's words: God "sent down the same Spirit by whose power he had dispensed the Word, to complete his work by the efficacious confirmation of the Word" (*Institutes of the Christian Religion* 1.9.3). Illumination refers not to some mystical or causal effect that has nothing to do with textual meaning, then, but to the right and proper outcome of biblical discourse: the understanding of faith. Calvin concurs: "Faith is the principal work of the Holy Spirit" (3.1.4), and the presence of faith—illumination—neither changes nor supplements the meaning of the text but rather enables those whom the Spirit illumines to recognize, feel, and respond to the meaning and force of what is written: "The Spirit [is] the inner teacher by whose effort the promise

51. Hall, *Reading Scripture with the Church Fathers*, 42.

52. See Barth, *Church Dogmatics*, 1.2:203–42; and Alston, *Illocutionary Acts and Sentence Meaning*, 31.

of salvation penetrates into our minds" (3.1.4). In short: what the Spirit does *through* the text is not unrelated to what the authors, human and divine, have done *in* it. As far as concerns the Spirit's speaking "through" Scripture, then, we might say that the *message* is the medium.

Scripture and Theodrama

Here ends my apology for authorial discourse interpretation. How has my mind changed since writing *Is There a Meaning in This Text?* Let me count the ways! Perhaps the most important change, at least for the purposes of the present essay, has to do with a growing recognition that my earlier account was too general and too formal (a polite way of saying *too abstract*). Stated more positively: I have come to see that biblical discourse is caught up in the very subject matter that it is about: the gospel of Jesus Christ. So, for that matter, is the attempt to interpret it. Scripture is a *script* that exists for the sake of interpreting the drama of redemption, and this in two senses: (1) the script records and makes sense of the divine action in the past, and (2) the script solicits the interpreter's participation in the ongoing action in the present.

The Norm: Scripted Theodrama

The gospel-centered subject matter of Scripture is (to borrow a term from von Balthasar) *theodramatic*: it is all about divine entrances and exoduses to and from the stage of world history. The plot culminates in the incarnation—God's unexpected entry into the form of humanity—and the crucifixion and "exodus" (= departure, death; see Luke 9:31) of Jesus Christ. The drama of redemption, like all dramas, is carried along by dialogical action: by the words of God, the Word who was God, and the words of the Word.[53] God's speech and God's deeds are the primary impulse behind the theodrama, the force that propels the action forward. Scripture not only depicts God's speech and action but is itself a result of these same divine communicative

53. For a discussion of how the words of Jesus bespeak Jesus's identity as the Word of God, see Robert H. Gundry, *Jesus the Word according to John the Sectarian* (Grand Rapids: Eerdmans, 2002), 1–50.

initiatives.[54] Scripture serves the theodrama by taking on the servant form of human language and literature.[55]

This newer focus on theodramatic subject matter complements my earlier focus on authorial discourse. Indeed, to the extent that discourse is implicitly dramatic—a matter of doing things by saying things—my earlier focus on divine authorial discourse was already theodramatic. What remains constant, then, between earlier and later Vanhoozer is the emphasis on the Spirit speaking in the Scriptures. However, I now recognize the equal importance of dealing with the other dimensions of biblical discourse (*"to* someone *about* something"). I also recognize how important it is to situate Scripture and theological hermeneutics in the context of the broader theodrama and hence to sort out the relative standing (status) of authors, text, reader, and subject matter, as the following three points make clear.

The first point concerns the relative status of the text and its subject matter. I agree with Barth that the method of theology should be appropriate to its matter (*Church Dogmatics* 1.1:1–24). The subject matter is *theodramatic*—God speaking, God doing—especially as this comes into focus in the word and act that is Jesus Christ: "God was in Christ reconciling the world to himself" (2 Cor. 5:19). The theodramatic action is covenantal, so, too, the theodramatic discourse.[56] Scripture sets forth what God has done as our God and what we are to do as his people. Scripture is the "servant form" of revelation (Bavinck), and revelation in turn serves the broader purpose of redemption. The Bible is less a system of ideas than it is a means of establishing and administering right covenantal relations. That certain rights and responsibilities are acquired in the course of author-

54. These points are treated in greater detail in Kevin J. Vanhoozer, *The Drama of Doctrine: A Canonical-Linguistic Approach to Christian Theology* (Louisville: Westminster/John Knox, 2005).

55. I am here amending Bavinck, who says that "Scripture is the servant form of revelation." I agree with Bavinck that Scripture is not an end in itself, but a means and instrument of God making all things new in Christ: Scripture is a "product of God's incarnation in Christ and in a sense its continuation, the way by which Christ makes his home in the church, the preparation of the way to the full indwelling of God." It is this indwelling of God in the people of God that is the goal: "Scripture, too, is a passing act"; Bavinck, *Reformed Dogmatics*, 1.380–81.

56. See Vanhoozer, "From Speech Acts to Scripture Acts," 159–203.

ing and interpreting the biblical discourse is therefore of the utmost significance. Everything in theological hermeneutics ultimately depends on ascribing and according the right status to the various communicants that Scripture brings together, not simply as communicants but also as participants in the theodramatic action, as we shall see below in our case study of Philemon.

The second point pertains to the relative status of the biblical text and the human and divine authors. I now want to insist that the theological interpretation of Scripture involves both reading the Bible like any other book—in doing justice to the authorial discourse—*and* reading the Bible *unlike* any other book, because (1) no other book bears divine authorial discourse; (2) no other book is the primary script of the theodrama; (3) no other book is so implicated in the triune economies of revelation and redemption; and (4) no other book is the medium for the self-presentation of Jesus Christ through the Spirit.[57]

The third point concerns the relative status of Scripture and the church as an interpretive community. What primarily makes the Bible "Scripture" is its being set apart by God for a special role in the broader economy of redemption and only secondarily its recognition as such in the church.[58] God is the divine playwright who providentially superintends the human authorial voices so that they express, even (and perhaps especially) in their diversity, the main plot of the redemptive action. Scripture is best viewed *sub specie theodramatis*: not only as a record of the theodrama but as a collection of voices that together communicate the main line of the redemptive action and invite readers to participate in its continuation.

The Bible thus holds a unique and authoritative place in the triune economy of salvation. I want to say of the doctrine of Scripture something similar to what Gustaf Aulén says about the doctrine of the atonement, and for much the same reasons. In his well-known book *Christus Victor*, Aulén contrasts what he calls the "dramatic" or classic view of the atonement with

57. See John Webster, *Word and Church: Essays in Christian Dogmatics* (Edinburgh: T&T Clark, 2001), 110.
58. See Webster, *Holy Scripture*.

the "objective" and "subjective" views.[59] According to Irenaeus's dramatic view, Christ's victory on the cross over death, depravity, and the devil is the means by which God reconciles all things to himself. The doctrine of Scripture, like the doctrine of atonement, has also been held hostage, at least in modernity, by a similar conservative-versus-liberal polarization. Conservatives emphasize the objective aspect of revelation, which views the Bible as a deposit of divinely revealed propositions; liberals emphasize the subjective aspect of revelation, which views the Bible as an expression of human religious experience.[60]

A theodramatic doctrine of Scripture centered on divine discourse (what God says about Christ to the church in the medium of human discourse), by contrast, emphasizes *intersubjectivity* (dialogue, communicative interaction): both the interpersonal interaction of the Spirit of God with the human authors of the Bible (inspiration) and the interpersonal interaction of the Spirit of God with the human readers of the Bible (illumination). Something like the notion of the Bible as divine discourse is, I believe, the "classic" position, the dominant idea in Scripture and in early church tradition.[61] Call it *Christus locutor*: the idea that Scripture is ultimately the Son's own Spirit-borne commissioned testimony to himself, the means by which Christ exercises his lordship over the church.[62]

59. In Aulén's schema, the Anselmian objective view understands Christ's work as directed at God (i.e., changing God's attitude toward humanity by satisfying God's honor, wrath, or justice), whereas the Abelardian subjective view understands Christ's work as directed at humanity (i.e., changing one's attitude toward God); see Gustaf Aulén, *Christus Victor: An Historical Study of the Three Main Types of the Idea of the Atonement* (New York: Macmillan, 1969), 1–3.

60. See Nancy Murphy, *Beyond Liberalism and Fundamentalism: How Modern and Postmodern Philosophy Set the Theological Agenda* (Valley Forge, PA: Trinity, 1996).

61. There is even some overlap between the causes of neglect of the classic idea of atonement and the reasons for the eclipse of what I call the dramatic idea of Scripture. Consider the following two parallels: (1) the polemical background of modern discussions and the polarization between the objective and subjective views, and (2) the dramatic view is not rational enough for the conservatives and too mythological for the liberals. See the discussion of how this affects the doctrine of atonement in Aulén, *Christus Victor*, 7–12.

62. To take the Bible as Scripture is to acknowledge "the self-bestowing presence of the risen Christ"; Webster, *Word and Church*, 35. For an account of Christ's lordship over the canon in terms of his messianic offices of prophet, priest, and king, see Vanhoozer, *Drama of Doctrine*, 196.

The triune communicative action continues beyond the original composition of the biblical texts. The gospel attested in the word written remains normative, yet the Spirit's subsequent work in the church—ministering the word, bringing about understanding, in a word, *illumining*—is also part of the economy of communicative action. I am evangelical because I am committed to the authority of the gospel in its canonical context; I am catholic because I recognize the Spirit's work in the church's reception of the gospel over the centuries and across cultures. It is the Spirit's speaking in and through Scripture that employs the authorial discourse, ministers the christological subject matter, and enables the ecclesial community's right reception.[63]

Theological Interpretation: Theodramatic Understanding

Theological hermeneutics is a matter, first, of grasping the basic plot—of being able to relate the various scenes in the theodrama to what God has done climactically in Jesus Christ—and, second, of grasping how we can go on following Christ in new situations so that our speech and action corresponds to the truth of the gospel. Theological hermeneutics is, in a word, a matter of theodramatic competence: the theological interpreter knows how to make sense of the drama of redemption both in terms of the biblical text and in terms of the contemporary experience of the church.

The purpose of theology is to facilitate our participation in the ongoing evangelical action: to equip us to be *doers* of the word, *imitators* of the disciples and apostles, and, at the limit, to help us create an ecclesially embodied argument for the truth of Jesus Christ. Doctrine is a vital aid in the theological interpretation of the Bible. Doctrine involves more than learning by rote a set of abstract truths. On the contrary, *doctrine is direction for the church's fitting participation in the ongoing drama of redemption.* Doctrine helps us both to identify the main *dramatis personae* (the Triune God, the human creature)

---

63. I largely agree with Fowl about the importance of Christian recovery of the habits and practices required to read the Bible within the overall plot of God's economy of salvation, though I identify the primary locus of these habits and practices in Scripture itself and only secondarily in the rule of faith.

and to understand the basic theodramatic plot (creation, fall, redemption).[64]

Theology, as "faith seeking theodramatic understanding," thus has two aspects: grasping the meaning of the script and discerning how to follow its directions in the contemporary situation. Theology therefore resembles both a *scientia* that employs exegetical disciplines in order to be faithful to the canonical text and a *sapientia* that enables disciples to perform their script in ways fitting to the present cultural context. The ultimate goal of theological interpretation of Scripture is *wisdom*: the ability to say and do what is Christianly fitting given our authoritative script and our cultural setting.

As to the truth of our interpretations, this is a matter of theodramatic "fit" or correspondence between God's words and deeds and our words and deeds, between God's understanding and ours. Though the climax of the theodrama—the death and resurrection of Jesus—is already past, the drama continues; hence truth is a matter of eschatological correspondence to the already/not-yet contours of the theodrama. On the one hand, truth names the *already* corresponding nature of the relation of doctrine to the theodrama. On the other hand, doctrine is also about what God is now doing through the Spirit and so articulates the *not yet* aspect of truth by directing us to *become* what we already *are*: creatures made new "in Christ."

Interpreting Philemon: Three Characters in Search of a Theodrama

The proof is in the pudding or, in this case, the *performance*. How shall we demonstrate our understanding of what God is saying to the church in and through Paul's discourse—the book of Philemon—today? Paul's is an important voice in the canon, and Philemon occupies a significant place in the theodramatic play-script. So, what do we get, as people of faith, if our search for understanding Philemon is successful? Christian wisdom.

64. For further development of this point, see Vanhoozer, *Drama of Doctrine*, chap. 3.

Philemon's Big Idea: Fitting Participation in the Theodrama

If its reception in the fourth century is any indication, Philemon makes a poor case study for theological hermeneutics: "This letter taught them nothing about questions of theological interest, nothing about matters of ecclesiastical discipline."[65] Some apparently suggested that if the letter were indeed Pauline, he must have written it at a time when he was bereft of the Spirit! John Chrysostom was at last able to find a *moral* message in Philemon: do not give up on even the most unpromising people. Many interpreters since Chrysostom follow him in reading Philemon as a case study in Christian morality.

Is there anything that resembles Christian *doctrine* in this letter? If not, why should theologians bother with it? The way forward is to recall our definition of doctrine as direction for our fitting participation in the ongoing theodrama and then to relate Paul's master/slave discourse to the dramatic action. Since we do not share Philemon's situation—not unless we are slave owners, that is—does it follow that Philemon speaks only to 1860s America? Not at all, for though we do not share Philemon's historical situation, we do share his *eschatological* situation: the church today is, like Philemon's, living between the times, between the first and second advents of Christ. Hence my thesis: Philemon is indeed theological in its concern for what it means to be "in Christ" (e.g., a new creation) and for what kind of *doing* naturally follows from that kind of *being*.

Status

The letter, theologically interpreted, is all about *status*. As such, it is of direct material and formal import to our topic: theological hermeneutics. Status, after all, has to do with one's "standing" in relation to others; the interpreter is one who *understands*.[66]

---

65. J. B. Lightfoot, *Saint Paul's Epistles to the Colossians and to Philemon* (1879; repr. Grand Rapids: Zondervan, 1959), 316–17.

66. Wayne Booth speaks of interpreters who "overstand" a text by approaching it with questions that reflect their own, rather than the text's, interests; see *Critical Understanding: The Powers and Limits of Pluralism* (Chicago: University of Chicago Press, 1979), 235–56.

Status pertains to one's position or rank in society, to one's standing in relation to others. In a broad sense, status has to do with one's value and importance in the eyes of the world: with being a somebody rather than a nobody. In a narrower sense, it has to do with one's legal standing with regard to some situation. Different societies have awarded status to different groups: warriors, priests, knights, poets, academics (not often), entertainers (more often). It is a truth universally acknowledged, as even Jane Austen knew, that a single man (or woman) must be in want of status, or at least a status symbol, such as a spouse.

In his fascinating and insightful book *Status Anxiety*, Alain de Botton makes a convincing case that the worry that we do not measure up, either in the eyes of our neighbors or in the opinion of society, is a cancer in the deepest recesses of our hearts and souls.[67] We crave recognition by others so that we can accept ourselves. I do not think Paul suffers from status anxiety (for reasons that will soon become apparent), but I do think he is seriously concerned over the status of Onesimus, particularly in the eyes of Philemon.

De Botton believes that we too often allow the sense of our own identity to be "held captive by the judgments of those we live among."[68] He therefore considers possible solutions to status anxiety. Philosophy, for example, helps us to see that others' opinions of us may not be accurate. Indeed, "public opinion is the worst of all opinions."[69] De Botton's final answer to status anxiety is "bohemia," that countercultural movement made up of socially unconventional artists and writers.[70] Bohemians do not give a fig for social opinion; they care more about their poetry and music and friends than status symbols. Indeed, some prefer poetic poverty to what they considered soul-destroying factory jobs or middle-class occupations. De Botton sees bohemia as an emotional substitute for the church and its emphasis on a spiritual status: "Like Christianity's monasteries and nunneries, bohemia's garrets, cafés, low-rent

67. Alain de Botton, *Status Anxiety* (New York: Pantheon, 2004).
68. Ibid., 8.
69. Sebastien Chamfort, cited in ibid., 116.
70. De Botton calls it a "democratic church" that despises the social conventions of the bourgeoisie. Bohemia "is not a place but an attitude of mind" (ibid., 267, citing Arthur Ransome, *Bohemia in London* [1907]).

districts and cooperative businesses have provided a refuge where that part of the population which is uninterested in pursuing the bourgeoisie's rewards . . . may find sustenance and fellowship."[71]

This is where the apostle Paul steps in to correct de Botton, adding to the solutions of Athens and bohemia the response of Jerusalem, for de Botton ignores the crucial role of justification by grace through faith, namely, the question of one's standing before God.[72] The gospel responds to status anxiety at the most profound level: one's relation to God. The good news is that we do not have to acquire status for ourselves; thanks to the work of Christ, we have a new status—a new legal standing—before God. Those who were once strangers and aliens to God have been adopted into his family. Adoption is the operative concept, conjoining as it does both legal and relational status.

Improvisation

Let me put one more element in place before turning to Philemon. Lived theological interpretation involves improvisation, which is not about being clever or original so much as joining in the stream of the action in an "obvious" and "fitting" way.

The genuine improviser trains herself "to act from habit in ways appropriate to the circumstance."[73] But this is precisely the task of discipleship: to find ways of staying faithful to our script in the midst of constantly changing circumstances. Jeremy Begbie describes the action in the book of Acts as "a stream of new, unpredictable, improvisations."[74] The Bible not only depicts such acts of apostolic improvisation but also trains

71. De Botton, *Status Anxiety*, 291–92.
72. De Botton does have a chapter on religion and makes two points: (1) religion reminds us of our finitude (and death) and so helps us to put questions of our social status in a broader perspective; and (2) Christianity introduces a second type of status—the spiritual—that is wholly unrelated to one's earthly status.
73. Samuel Wells, *Improvisation: The Drama of Christian Ethics* (Grand Rapids: Brazos, 2004), 65.
74. Jeremy Begbie, *Theology, Music, and Time* (Cambridge: Cambridge University Press), 222–23.

us, by cultivating habits of the mind and habits of the heart, to participate faithfully yet creatively in the ongoing drama of redemption.

As theologians of liberation rightly remind us, doctrine should not simply be left idling in the mind; it should generate right action. I agree. Doctrine in my view is direction for the disciple's fitting participation in the triune action, particularly in the missions of the Son and the Spirit. And this brings us back to status.

The present theodramatic scene is focused on the church, and that means, to use Bonhoeffer's term, "life together." Life together is a matter of interpersonal interaction, and every personal interaction invites us to treat others either as superiors, inferiors, or equals. Improvisers are taught to recognize status, for "status informs *every single interaction between people*."[75] Status is not something one has; it is something one *does*.[76] Virtually every word or gesture we make implies something about our status. One may be low in social status, but you can "play high" and try to dominate; Charlie Chaplin's tramp may be low in social status, but he puts on gentleman-like airs.

Most of us are experts in guarding our status; we are uncomfortable acting either lower or higher than we think we really are. Most people will do almost anything to remain in their preferred positions, the part they know best. Part of the fun in improvisation is to see what happens with respect to status transactions. Keith Johnstone speaks of the "see-saw" principle: "I go up and you go down."[77] And the one see-saw status transaction that gives the most pleasure to audiences involves the master/servant relation.[78] In the words of one writer on improvisation, the best play "is one which ingeniously displays and reverses the status between the characters."[79] With this thought in mind, let us now turn to Paul's letter to Philemon, a discourse about what a Christian should do when a runaway slave repents and returns to his or her master.

75. Wells, *Improvisation*, 88 (italics original).
76. Keith Johnstone, *Impro: Improvisation and the Theatre* (New York: Routledge, 1981), 36.
77. Ibid., 37.
78. Ibid., 62.
79. Ibid., 72.

A Reading of Philemon

The Occasion: The World behind the Text and the Story Thus Far (1–7)

Historical research into the nature of slavery in the first century takes us only so far in illumining the meaning of Philemon.[80] All we really know is that Onesimus is AWOL and that Paul has decided to intercede on his behalf.[81] It is for this reason that quests for the historical Onesimus (some believe he is the same Onesimus who later became bishop of Ephesus) are largely irrelevant for the understanding of Philemon.[82] What we need to know about Onesimus we can get from the text, namely, that he represents "the least respectable type of the least respectable class in the social scale."[83] His status is the lowest of the low.

Interestingly, Paul himself stakes out a low status position at the very beginning of his epistle, foregoing the usual designation *apostle* in favor of "Paul, a prisoner for Christ Jesus" (1). From the opening line, then, Paul sends the reader important status signals.[84] In verses 4–7 Paul focuses on Philemon's love, a love that spontaneously gushes forth and that has already refreshed the hearts of the saints. Verse 6 contains the key phrase (and also, according to C. F. D. Moule,[85] the most obscure), the "sharing" or *koinōnia* of Philemon's faith that will serve as the basis of Paul's ensuing plea on behalf of Onesimus. Some commentators view the phrase *koinōnia*

80. *Pace* John M. G. Barclay, *Colossians and Philemon* (Sheffield: Sheffield Academic Press, 1997), 97.

81. So Lightfoot: "All that we really know of Philemon is contained within this epistle itself"; *Philemon*, 306.

82. This is also why I leave to one side John Knox's argument that the real recipient of the letter is not Philemon but Archippus; *Philemon among the Letters of Paul* (London: Collins, 1960), 49–61. I agree with Edward Lohse that Knox fails to observe "the methodological rule of first trying to understand a writing in the light of its own statements before drawing on other documents for purposes of comparison"; *Colossians and Philemon* (Philadelphia: Fortress, 1971), 187.

83. Lightfoot, *Philemon*, 311.

84. Lohse comments that Paul's status as a prisoner of Christ actually elevates his apostolic status and indicates that "this writing should not be taken as a mere private letter. It conveys a message that obligates its recipients to obey the apostolic word"; *Colossians and Philemon*, 189.

85. C. F. D. Moule, *The Epistles to the Colossians and to Philemon* (Cambridge: Cambridge University Press, 1957), 142.

of faith as referring to Philemon's "faith-communion with Christ."[86] Others give it an active sense: "generosity."[87] *Koinōnia* is the saintly spontaneity typical of those who participate "in Christ."[88] In any case, Paul prays that the *koinōnia* of Philemon's faith—"the kindly deeds of charity which spring from your faith"[89]—would lead to a "knowledge" or "recognition" of *the good in Christ*. What is in view here is what we might call the *disciples' performance knowledge* of our union with Christ.

The Offer (8–20) and the World of the Text

Paul's plea, the longest part of the letter, begins with "therefore" (or "accordingly") in verse 8. This is crucial; improvisers never begin with a blank slate but with a premise. The good improviser does not go off on his or her own tangent—does not "script-write"—but continues the preceding action in an appropriate, though often surprising, manner.

Paul's own style of discourse is consistent with his message. He does not lord it over Philemon (though as an apostle, he could) but instead makes an offer: "Accordingly, though I am bold enough in Christ to command you to do what is required, yet for love's sake I prefer to appeal to you" (8). An "offer," in the context of improvisation, refers to anything one actor says or does to another. Paul's offer is his sending Onesimus back and his asking Philemon to do *to anēkon*—"what is required" or, even better, "what is fitting" under the circumstances—which is to say, in the context of the new creation "in Christ" (cf. Col. 3:18).

Paul's request, and the epistle as a whole, is all about status transactions, about rethinking interpersonal relationships in light of our relation to Christ. In a scant twenty-five verses, the main characters change roles and assume each other's identities as frequently as in a Shakespearean comedy! Consider: Paul is clearly Philemon's superior but refrains from invoking his apostolic authority and "commanding" Philemon (8). Onesimus

86. Ibid., 142.
87. Peter T. O'Brien, *Colossians, Philemon* (Word Biblical Commentary 44; Waco: Word, 1982), 280.
88. Cf. Lohse, *Colossians and Philemon*, 193, who cites 1 Cor. 10:16–17 as a parallel.
89. Lightfoot, *Philemon*, 335.

is Philemon's slave but Paul's begotten or adopted "son" (10), a rank of an altogether different status. Paul goes further, identifying Onesimus as his brother (16) and his very heart (12). Paul wants to keep Onesimus with him so that he could serve Paul on Philemon's behalf (13). So: Onesimus plays Philemon's role for Paul and takes on Paul's identity for Philemon. Hence the core request: "receive him . . . as me" (17).[90] Paul here identifies Onesimus with himself, a move that Luther sees as parallel to Christ's taking our part in order to reconcile us with God.

Paul is asking Philemon, someone with high social status, to receive Onesimus "no longer as a slave but as more than a slave, as a beloved brother" (16). *The whole epistle turns upon Philemon's recognizing what is fitting for him to do with regard to Onesimus given their mutual adoption into the family of God "in Christ."* The *koinōnia* of faith that serves as the basis of Paul's appeal is nothing less than the company of the gospel, the community of fellow players in the theodrama. Paul is saying to Philemon: keep on playing your part in the divine comedy of redemption as well as you have been playing it up to now.

Offers can be accepted or blocked: "A block is anything that prevents the action from developing, or that wipes out your partner's premise."[91] Paul's premise is nothing less than Christ's resurrection: there is a new creation; all things have become new. His offer to Philemon consists in his asking Philemon to act on just this premise, not "by compulsion" but in a way that is spontaneous (*hekousion*) (14). The real issue in the letter is whether Philemon will accept Onesimus's changed status: "It is this *category change* which Paul expects to make all the difference."[92] Onesimus *is* more than a slave for those with the theodramatic imagination to see the new order of things in Christ.

The Outcome: Accepting (21–25) and the World in front of the Text

Paul is confident of Philemon's "obedience"—a strange term to use given the appeal to Philemon's *koinōnia* in the faith and

90. "The emphatic ἐγώ [in verse 20] identifies the cause of Onesimus with his own"; ibid., 344.
91. Johnstone, *Impro*, 97.
92. Barclay, *Colossians and Philemon*, 110.

spontaneous love.[93] Here we begin to see that the master/slave dichotomy may not exhaust all the options—that there may be a kind of obedience that is not only compatible with but of the essence of Christian freedom. What exactly does Paul expect Philemon to do? Some commentators think that Paul's reference to Philemon's doing "even more than I say" (21) was his way of making a veiled request for Onesimus's manumission. Others say Paul *would* have made such a request had the sociopolitical circumstances allowed. Still others—John Barclay, for instance—are disappointed by Paul's silence. How could he not have criticized such a blatant example of social injustice as the institution of slavery?[94] Interestingly, both sides of the nineteenth-century debate over slavery used Philemon. The question is this: which side accepted Paul's offer and which blocked it?

There is every reason to think that Philemon honored Paul's request. Paul himself is clearly confident of a happy ending. Philemon may thus be read as an apostolic comedy, for "a comedian is someone paid to lower his own or other people's status."[95] Paul is an agent of divine comedy, a radical improviser who wreaks havoc on conventional status hierarchies by calling readers to turn the status categories of the world upside down as they participate in the world projected by the gospel. Standing behind Paul's call for evangelical improvisation is nothing less than a prevenient divine improvisation, namely, the incarnation of the Son. Johnstone comments: "A great play is a virtuoso display of status transactions."[96] Well, there is no greater display of a reversal in status than Philippians 2:6–7: "Who, being in very nature God, did not consider equality with God something to be grasped, but made himself nothing, taking the very nature of a servant." It is Luther who spots the *cantus firmus* of embodied improvisations of Christian love: "What Christ has done for us with God the Father, that St. Paul does also for Onesimus with Philemon."[97]

93. O'Brien notes that Paul uses the same term to speak of Christ's obedience to God in Rom. 5:19, an obedience freely given; *Colossians, Philemon*, 305.
94. Barclay, *Colossians and Philemon*, 125.
95. Johnstone, *Impro*, 39.
96. Ibid., 72.
97. Martin Luther, "Preface to the Epistle of Saint Paul to Philemon, 1546 (1522)," in *Luther's Works* (ed. E. Theodore Bachmann; Philadelphia: Fortress, 1960), 35.390.

Pauline Faith Seeking Performance Understanding

Some interpreters find Paul capitulating to the status quo in a disappointing way. How else could Jerome appeal to Philemon to defend slavery, and why else would Luther say that Paul was not advocating abolitionism but simply the reconciliation of slave and master? Does Paul operate with a dualism between the spiritual and the social? Should we?

Philemon is not primarily an ethical treatise, but a key scene in an all-encompassing theodrama. Attempts to portray Paul as sanctioning slavery are guilty of unsportsmanlike conduct, for Paul is not intending here to lay down a developed social ethic.[98] On the contrary, he is making Philemon an *eschatological* offer that he cannot refuse, an offer that nevertheless carries concrete ethical implications.[99] Just as Philemon's love has *already* refreshed Paul's heart, so Paul expects that there is a "not yet" and "how much more" aspect to Philemon's love that will refresh his heart again (20).

Paul is expecting Philemon to act in a "more" than ethical way (21: "knowing that you will do even more than I say"). This "even more" is first cousin to the eschatological "how much more" of Romans 5. Paul's "offer" thus partakes of a kind of "eschatological suspension of the ethical." Paul expects Philemon to go on living *sub specie theodramatis*—"under the perspective of the theodrama." It is in this perspective that Philemon is to see Onesimus as "more than a slave, as a beloved brother" (16).

Lohse is right: "The letter to Philemon is neither the disguise of a general idea nor the promulgation of a generally valid rule about the question of slavery."[100] It is rather a concrete communicative act of evangelical wisdom. But it need not follow that it has nothing to say to us today about the shape our life together should take. Theological interpreters are apprentices to Phile-

98. Paul's statements about slavery in 1 Cor. 7:20–23 also seem to encourage his readers to adopt a theodramatic perspective.

99. Philemon cannot refuse Paul's offer, that is, and remain true to his new nature. Because Philemon has already given evidence of his new nature, however, Paul is confident that Philemon will react spontaneously, do what is obvious (to those "in Christ"), and hence improvise with creative fidelity.

100. Lohse, *Colossians and Philemon*, 188.

mon. By keeping company with Philemon, we can learn the same habit of Christian practical wisdom called for (and expected) by Paul. The same fundamental judgment about a person's status in Christ can, and must, be applied in any number of concrete social contexts.[101]

So, does Paul expect only the company of the gospel to be status reversers, and to do so only in the confines of the church, or should the church work to change the very status structures of society?[102] Is our status as creatures of God and brothers and sisters of Christ "purely abstract or ethereal . . . without practical impact on daily life"?[103] Lightfoot may have had it right: "When . . . the Apostolic precept that 'in Christ is neither bond nor free' was not only recognised but acted upon, then slavery was doomed. Henceforward it was only a question of time."[104] The point is that Philemon presents the church with an apostolic offer that, if accepted, works itself out with inexorable theodramatic logic. The church is a leaven in the social lump; our already/not-yet status "in Christ" is the firstfruit of what will one day be universal history: "every knee shall bow" (Rom. 14:11; cf. Isa. 45:23).

At the end of the day, to insist that Philemon is "about slavery" is (ironically enough) to *limit* its "usefulness." Paul's offer to Philemon is an even more radical, and universal, message than one that concerns masters and slaves only. It concerns all of us: the church is a company of gospel players whose status is determined by their place "in Christ." While we may still choose to play high or low status toward one another, the truth of the matter is that all our social status symbols have been overturned. The symbols of our gospel status are the waters of baptism, the bread and the wine. God has overturned the status wisdom of the world.

101. This may be the practical equivalent of David Yeago's contention that the same judgment may be rendered by a variety of different concepts; see "The New Testament and the Nicene Dogma: A Contribution to the Recovery of Theological Exegesis," in *The Theological Interpretation of Scripture* (ed. Stephen E. Fowl; Oxford: Blackwell, 1997), 87–100.

102. I am indebted to Dan Treier for forcing me to deal with this important question.

103. Barclay, *Colossians and Philemon*, 116.

104. Lightfoot, *Philemon*, 325.

Conclusion: Status and Improvisation in Theological Interpretation

In this essay I have examined how our status in Christ ought to govern our status transactions with others. But what of the status of the theological interpreter vis-à-vis the biblical text? It remains only to ascertain the relative status of author, text, subject matter, and reader in light of Paul's subversion of the master/slave dichotomy itself. Instead of asking, "Which is to be the slave and which the master?" we need to recover Paul's notion of understanding as free obedience, for in the final analysis, theological interpretation of Scripture is itself theodramatic: a matter of how the finite freedom of the interpreting community (viz., the church) will respond to what Karl Barth calls the absolute freedom of Holy Scripture in which the former is grounded (*Church Dogmatics* 1.2 §21: "Freedom in the Church").

Philemon is a small but powerful scene of theodramatic understanding, a paradigmatic instance of hermeneutic parenesis[105] that depicts how a reader (viz., Philemon) with theodramatic understanding ought to respond to apostolic (viz., Paul's) discourse. In this key theological hermeneutical scene, then, Paul stands in for the author, Philemon for the reader. And what of Onesimus? As a slave, Onesimus has virtually no claim on Philemon. This corresponds to what Morgan said about texts: "Texts have no aims, no rights."[106] Onesimus, then, has the status of a text. To be precise, he is the embodiment of Paul's discourse: a living letter, something "sent" from someone to someone (12), Paul's "child" (10), Paul's heart (12), an extension of Paul himself. Moreover, just as Scripture is "profitable" for teaching and correction when received the right way (2 Tim. 3:16), so Onesimus is "useful" to Philemon (11), provided that Philemon receive him "no longer as a slave" (16).

I do not wish to allegorize here and make Paul say something *other* than what he is saying. I am rather concerned to read Philemon as a paradigm of how to interpret, receive, and "perform" apostolic discourse. To be precise, I am reading Philemon as,

105. In the context of New Testament ethics, *parainesis* is the technical Greek term (meaning "advice") for moral exhortation concerning a number of perennial practical issues of living.

106. Morgan, *Biblical Interpretation*, 7.

among other things, a metaphorical lesson in theological interpretation of Scripture. According to Richard Hays, the task of
hermeneutical appropriation often requires just such a creative
appropriation: "Whenever we appeal to the authority of the New
Testament, we are necessarily engaged in metaphor-making,
placing our community's life imaginatively within the world
articulated by the texts."[107]

Hays's fourfold task of New Testament ethics, when brought
to bear on the ethics of interpreting apostolic discourse, conveniently serves to illumine the fourfold task of theological interpretation of Scripture.[108] My reading of Philemon moves through
all four stages:

1. The descriptive task of reading the text carefully: my exegesis of Philemon seeks to highlight the distinctive *hermeneutical* vision (e.g., theodramatic understanding) embodied
   in the text.
2. The synthetic task of placing the text in canonical context:
   Hays's own choice of focal images—community, cross,
   and new creation—works well here too. I argue that Philemon is a word to the Christian community about the
   cross of Christ that makes all things—especially status
   relations—new.
3. The hermeneutical task of relating the text to our situation: I suggest that Philemon is a metaphorical depiction
   of what goes on in theological interpretation of Scripture.
   The church today needs to learn to receive the prophetic
   and apostolic discourse about the new creation in Christ,
   just as Philemon did.
4. The pragmatic task of living the text: the final task of theological hermeneutics is that of embodying or *performing*
   the Scriptures. The present essay not only issues a clarion
   call to obedient and faithful performance but attempts to
   exemplify such performance in its reading of Philemon.

We can best appreciate the radicality of Paul's distinct Christian
theological understanding of interpretive freedom—improvisation

107. Hays, *Moral Vision of the New Testament*, 6.
108. See ibid., 3–7.

with an authoritative script—when we set it beside more secular, philosophical views. As we have seen, a faulty anthropology (e.g., the master/slave dualism) holds both Hegel and Nietzsche, and perhaps most moderns and postmoderns, captive.[109] The better way to determine the status of the interpreter vis-à-vis Scripture (and its author) is to view both in theodramatic context. If Nietzsche had done so, he would have seen that human beings are creatures, not creators, yet creatures with freedom and dignity. He might also have seen a viable alternative to the dichotomy of slave and master, namely, the willing servant. This, I suggest, is the better metaphor for the Christian interpreter of Scripture.

George Steiner pictures the interpreter as a hospitable host who serves—or, why not say it? *ministers*—the text. Good service is hard to find; texts are more often used than welcomed and served. Steiner helpfully identifies four stages in the process of interpretation:[110] (1) interpretation begins in trust that there is something in the text worth considering and understanding; (2) the second stage consists of a "raid" on the text, invading it with our questions, analytic techniques, exegetical procedures, and concerns; (3) we bring it home and domesticate it within our own system of thinking; (4) like Nietzsche, too many interpreters stop at the third stage, but for Steiner, there is a fourth stage: an act of restitution, a recognition that what the author wrote has a kind of independent integrity. The best interpretations attain this fourth stage and, in so doing, *allow the text to come into its own in our context*. It is the humble-hearted rather than swollen-headed reader who practices such hermeneutic hospitality. And this brings us back to Paul and theological hermeneutics.

Theological hermeneutics proceeds not from the Hegelian *Geist* but from the *Heilige Geist* (the Holy Spirit), and that means *ascertaining the status of the theological interpreter vis-à-vis the*

109. Hans-Georg Gadamer and Paul Ricoeur are exceptions to the rule. They are more concerned to expose themselves to the effect of the text than to treat the text like an inert object, more prone to appropriate than to assimilate. My own view, however, is that their hermeneutics are exceptions precisely because they employ theological categories (e.g., miracle, revelation, disclosure). In the final analysis, though, such theological categories enjoy only notional, not operational, "status" in philosophical hermeneutics. For a further elaboration of this point, see Vanhoozer, "Discourse on Matter."

110. See George Steiner, *After Babel: Aspects of Language and Translation* (London: Oxford University Press, 1975), 300–302.

text not from dialectics but rather from eschatology—to be precise, from our new status "in Christ." When we do so, we see what is missing in the master/slave dichotomy: not only the theme of service, but also that of grace, together with the *koinōnia* of faith that spontaneously erupts in works of love.

In the Gospel of Mark, the disciples do not recognize who Jesus is because they want to be great (high status). Jesus tells them that they must become like a child (low status). Jesus also says in John 13:16 that "a servant is not greater than his master." While our status toward one another may be that of brother and sister as befits those who are children of God, our status toward the covenant Lord is that of covenant servant: "Especially in theological hermeneutics, understanding is not the mastery of a text but service to the *Sache* of the text."[111]

Here we may recall what Calvin says about the main virtues of the commentator being brevity and lucidity. The biblical interpreter must get out of the way, as it were, so that readers can engage the word of God.[112] In the words of N. T. Wright: "Theological interpretation of Scripture needs constantly to remind itself that we know what true theology is, just as we know who the true God is, by looking at what it means to take the form of a servant."[113]

Interpreting Scripture theologically involves more than employing the right methods; it is a matter of cultivating the right virtues, virtues commensurate with the status of the interpreter-servant in relation to the scriptural text. The most important virtue is humility: the willingness to assume a lower status, to serve and attend others—authors—as greater than oneself. Biblical interpretation is ultimately a spiritual affair that demands a certain "mortification"[114] of the reader. What is conspicuously absent in the contemporary scene are self-effacing, humble-hearted readers, who do not consider equality with the author "something to be grasped but make themselves nothing, taking the form of a servant" (Phil. 2:7).

111. Philippe Eberhard, *The Middle Voice in Gadamer's Hermeneutics* (Tübingen: Mohr, 2004), 188.

112. Calvin, *Calvin: Commentaries* (Philadelphia: Westminster, 1958), 73.

113. N. T. Wright, "Philippians, Book of," in *Dictionary for the Theological Interpretation of the Bible* (ed. Kevin J. Vanhoozer et al.; Grand Rapids: Baker, 2005), 590.

114. So Webster, *Word and Church*, 81.

There is neither drudgery nor lack of dignity in serving Scripture. On the contrary, to serve the text is not only to witness to its good news but also to embody it. Such service is neither slavery nor mastery, but obedient (and responsible) freedom. Barth puts it like this: "This readiness and willingness to make one's own the responsibility for understanding the Word of God is freedom under the Word" (*Church Dogmatics* 1.2.696). The final word on the status of the theological interpreter, however, belongs to joy, for *theodramatic understanding as illustrated in Philemon is the glad recognition of and spontaneous response to another*. It is our privilege to be glad servants and joyful performers of the biblical text. There is no more contradiction between interpretive freedom and obedience to the Word than there is between Jesus's freedom and obedience to his Father.

It is therefore for free improvisation that Christ has set us free. When we act spontaneously according to our new natures, we are free indeed. Like Philemon, we demonstrate our understanding of the apostolic discourse that bears God's word, and of our status in Christ, by our fitting participation in the drama of redemption. Theological interpretation ultimately demands no less: an improvisation that is as free as it is faithful and that befits our new status in Christ and our new situation in the world. This is the kind of theological interpretation that the church so desperately needs: *dramatic* interpretations that *embody* the script and *refresh* the heart.

4

Are There Still Four Gospels?

A Study in Theological Hermeneutics

FRANCIS WATSON

Who is Jesus Christ? The answer to that question comprehends Christian faith in its entirety. An assertion is recognizably Christian only if it also entails an answer to the question of Jesus's identity. Christian talk about God is Christian only if God is understood in relation to Jesus, and Jesus in relation to God. Christian talk about the world is Christian only if the world is understood in its relation to Jesus and to the God whose triune being Jesus discloses. For Christian faith, the question of Jesus's identity is the question of all questions, on which all else hangs. Bound up in it are the all-comprehending questions of the identity of God and of the world.

Yet talk about Jesus refers us not to an abstract generalization but to a concrete particular. If Jesus represents the point at which the relation between God and the world is revealed and determined, that point still takes the form of a contingent historical existence, known to us like other historical contingencies in the traces it has left behind. These traces include written texts, notably the four parallel narrations of Jesus's ministry and its outcome known since early times as "gospels." If there is a comprehensive answer to the question of Jesus's identity, there is also a particular one, and this answer is very simple. Who is Jesus Christ? Answer: he is the protagonist of the fourfold gospel narration that bears the names of Matthew, Mark, Luke, and John. For Christian faith, Jesus is not encountered directly but is mediated through texts. Not only through texts, but also through community, through the neighbor, through bread and wine. Yet it is the texts themselves that specify these nontextual mediations. It is the evangelists' Jesus who promises his presence where two or three are gathered in his name; who identifies himself with the hungry and thirsty, with strangers and prisoners; and who gives his own body and blood in the forms of bread and wine. The canonical Gospels are not just a resource for the Christian community, highly valued but in the last resort dispensable or replaceable. On the contrary, they are fundamental to the church's existence.[1] If replaced by other texts, the outcome would be not only another Jesus but also another community. The community that sees God and the world in relation to Jesus is bound to Matthew, Mark, Luke, and John.

Why these four? Why not the *Gospel of Thomas* or Q or the *Protevangelium of James*, an appealing second-century text in which the birth of Jesus is set in the context of the birth and childhood of Mary, his mother? Why not the *Gospel of Mary*, a text in which the possibility that the Savior's profoundest revelations might be communicated through a woman is asserted and defended against the objections of patriarchal orthodoxy?

1. In opposition to such a claim, James Barr emphasizes that "Jesus in his teaching is nowhere portrayed as commanding or even sanctioning the production of a written Gospel, still less a written New Testament"; *Holy Scripture: Canon, Authority, Criticism* (Philadelphia: Westminster, 1983), 12. Over against liberal Protestant suspicion of Scripture as a category, the claim that the Gospels are basic to the church's existence would have to be elaborated by way of a trinitarian theology of divine self-communicative action—on which point see John Webster, *Word and Church: Essays in Christian Dogmatics* (Edinburgh: T&T Clark, 2001), 25–29.

If the Christian community learned to embrace such texts, it would no doubt be changed by them. But perhaps that would be a change for the better, a symbolic act of resistance to the patriarchal tendency that continues to disfigure the church's life. Is the insistence on the usual four Gospels anything more than a piece of unthinking conservatism, devoid of the Spirit? The inclusion of the excluded, the marginalized, and the silenced is a key demand of our current *Zeitgeist*, which seeks thereby to destabilize and deconstruct the totalitarian orthodoxies founded on an original act of exclusion. Arguably, the relation of canonical to so-called apocryphal gospels is a classic case of just such an act of exclusion. The canonizing of four Gospels is a repressive act that must be undone by attending to the voices it once silenced: that is the conviction underlying much of the current scholarly and popular interest in the apocryphal literature.[2] Put simply, the apocryphal must destabilize the canonical. The canonical boundary must be removed, depriving Matthew, Mark, Luke, and John of their privileged status and aligning them with Q, Thomas, Peter, and Mary. This program represents a further application of the hermeneutical principle that the Bible and its component parts should be "interpreted like any other book."[3]

In this essay, I shall argue that the canonical boundary is more important, and more interesting, than this program would suggest—concerned as it is with abstract power relations at the expense of concrete theological content. I shall offer an alternative rationale for the fourfold canonical gospel, drawing on theological resources bequeathed to us by the second century in order to reassert the validity and necessity of the canonical limit. Matthew, Mark, Luke, and John are not to be interpreted

2. For examples of this, see Elisabeth Schüssler Fiorenza, "Transgressing Canonical Boundaries," in *Searching the Scriptures*, vol. 2: *A Feminist Commentary* (ed. E. Schüssler Fiorenza; New York: Crossroad, 1994), 1–14; Helmut Koester, *Ancient Christian Gospels: Their History and Development* (Philadelphia: Trinity, 1990), 43–48; John Dominic Crossan, *The Birth of Christianity: Discovering What Happened in the Years Immediately Following the Execution of Jesus* (New York: HarperCollins, 1998), 407–22; and Bart D. Ehrman, *Lost Christianities: The Battles for Scripture and the Faiths We Never Knew* (Oxford: Oxford University Press, 2001), 229–57.

3. A principle classically enunciated by Benjamin Jowett, "On the Interpretation of Scripture," in *Essays and Reviews* (by F. Temple et al.; London: Parker, 1860), 330–433, at 377.

like any other gospel, because (as a matter of fact) they have not been so interpreted within the community of their catholic Christian readers, but also because, within this social context, privileged treatment is an appropriate response to these texts' distinctive characteristics. The fourfoldness of the church's canonical gospel is more than just a social fact. It has a theological rationale of its own.

Before turning to the second century, however, I shall offer an analysis of the anticanonical approach to the Gospels in its most influential contemporary guise. I refer to Dan Brown's novel, *The Da Vinci Code*. I should emphasize that I do not wish to suggest that serious scholarly advocacy of noncanonical gospels is in any way implicated in the distortions perpetrated by this ill-informed work.

The Appeal of the Apocryphal

Dan Brown's tale of codes and code-breakers has been so successful that even those who know they will not like it feel forced to read it, if only to be able to substantiate their dislike in the face of the novel's legion admirers.[4] Among other things, this is a work of popular theology, and its theology—or theological interpretation of church history—is a crucial element in its success. Parts of this theology are at least as old as the Reformation. We learn, once again, that church history is actually the history of a conspiracy in which the church's leaders successfully concealed the original revelation, substituting a religion that expressed their own will to power: Christianity as we know it. The task is therefore to unmask the conspiracy and to recover the holy grail that is the original revelation. The quest for the original revelation is an extraordinarily difficult task, since the conspiracy has so successfully covered its own tracks that almost everyone takes the substitute to be the real thing. *Almost* everyone, for there have always been a few enlightened souls to whom the truth was known and who managed to pass

4. Dan Brown, *The Da Vinci Code* (New York: Doubleday, 2003). At a recent graduation address at my own university, the excellence of this work was regarded as an established fact.

it on from one generation to the next, exposing themselves to the wrath of the all-powerful ecclesiastical institution in doing so. Early Protestants saw their own recovery of the holy grail as anticipated by Wycliffe, or Huss, or the author of the *Theologia germanica*. In Brown's retelling of this Protestant grail legend, the iconic figure is Leonardo da Vinci. At the heart of the book lies an interpretation of Leonardo's "Last Supper."

At first sight this painting looks orthodox enough. Jesus sits in the middle of the apostles, six to the left of him and six to the right. He has just announced that one of them is to betray him, and the painting captures the moment of the disciples' response, as they attempt to identify the betrayer. In Matthew and Mark, the disciples each in turn address themselves to Jesus: "Is it I?" (Matt. 26:22; Mark 14:19). These evangelists also draw attention to the disciples' sorrow. In Luke and John, however, the disciples turn in their uncertainty not to Jesus but to one another (Luke 22:23; John 13:22). Also in John, though not in Luke, the question "Lord, who is it?" is put to Jesus, on Simon Peter's initiative, by the disciple whom Jesus loved, as he reclines on Jesus's breast. Indeed, this is the moment when the fourth evangelist introduces the figure of the beloved disciple to the reader: "One of the disciples was reclining on Jesus's breast, the one whom Jesus loved. So Simon Peter made a sign to him and said to him, Who is it he is speaking of? So when he [the beloved disciple] had reclined on Jesus's chest, he said to him: Who is it?" (John 13:23–25 Vulgate).

Leonardo harmonizes these divergences between the canonical Gospels by dividing the apostles into four groups of three. The first and third groups, on the far left of the painting and to Jesus's immediate left, look toward Jesus himself and are asking: "Is it I?" They comprise Bartholomew, James son of Alphaeus, and Andrew in group 1, and Thomas, James son of Zebedee, and Philip in group 3. Their gestures express not only sorrow but also horror and incredulity. These disciples represent the Matthean and Markan account. On the far right of the painting, the three disciples comprising group 4 (Matthew, Thaddaeus, and Simon) look in their perplexity not to Jesus but to one another—in accordance with Luke and John. To Jesus's immediate right, Peter converses with John the beloved disciple, while Judas sits in silence and solitude: the three of them comprise group 2. John leans toward Peter, who has placed his hand on John's shoulder, drawing him away from Jesus and toward himself in order to ask, *sotto voce*, "Who is it he is speaking of?" This is the distinctively Johannine contribution to the painting. So Leonardo's division of the Twelve into four groups of three serves to harmonize the Gospels, with groups 1 and 3 playing a Matthean and Markan role, group 4 a Lukan and Johannine role, and group 2 an exclusively Johannine role. The four groups of disciples correspond roughly to the four Gospels. The painting seems to be a theologically orthodox rendering of the fourfold canonical text.[5]

Yet, for *The Da Vinci Code*, as for other conspiracy-theory renditions of church history, theological orthodoxy is nothing other than the repression of an original truth. Here, the achievement of Leonardo's "Last Supper" is that it depicts this act of repression in such a way that the repressed truth remains clearly visible to those with eyes to see. So what is this repressed truth? Well, to begin with, the figure who leans away from Jesus toward Peter is in fact *a woman* (Brown and his characters within the novel have in mind the beloved disciple's centrally parted hair, which flows down over the shoulders).[6] Leaning away from Jesus, she and Jesus create a V-shaped space that symbolizes (so we are told) both the eucharistic chalice and the female genitals.[7] And this V shape is also the hollow in the middle of the letter M created by the upper bodies of Jesus and the second group of his disciples: Judas, Peter, and (no longer John but) the unknown woman. What does this M mean? M is for Mary: the M-shaped disposition of the bodies reveals the unknown woman disciple to be Mary Magdalene, seated in the place of honor next to Jesus.[8] Peter's hand on her shoulder appears to threaten her.[9] We know from the *Gospel of Thomas* that Peter once said to Jesus, "Let Mary leave us, for women are not worthy of life" (*Gospel of Thomas* 114). We also know (or think we do) that the canonical Gospels were selected at the time of Constantine, when the

5. This interpretation of Leonardo's painting is my own. There is no indication in *The Da Vinci Code* that its author has read the canonical Gospels.

6. Brown, *Da Vinci Code*, 347. They also claim to be able to detect "delicate folded hands, and the hint of a bosom."

7. Ibid., 320–22.

8. Ibid., 328–30; here I simplify slightly.

9. Ibid., 334.

Christian church joined forces with Roman imperial power,[10] and that among the many alternative gospels that were then rejected was a *Gospel of Mary*. In this text, Mary represents the female principle of deity while Peter again represents a hostile patriarchal church, asking incredulously: "Did [the Savior] really speak privately with a woman, and not openly with us? Are we to turn about and all listen to her? Did he prefer her to us?" (*Gospel of Mary* 17.15–20).[11] Leonardo was heir to a secret tradition that handed down the holy grail, that is, the original truth of the eternal feminine incarnated in Mary—a truth that the imperial church and its successors were desperate to suppress.

Specialists in art history and in Christian origins will no doubt have rather serious reservations about much of this; for them, the only question is whether the errors and implausibilities stem from ignorance or from the novelist's license to invent.[12] What is more significant is that this construal of Christian history is apparently regarded as credible by many of the novel's nonspecialist readers. There is no mystery about why this is so. Within a deconstructive ethos, a conspiracy theory will always seem plausible—especially where the theory in question has a long pedigree within cultures shaped by Protestantism and the Enlightenment. Here, it is simply self-evident that Christian orthodoxy must have been founded on the suppression of an original truth that remains to be uncovered. If the four canonical Gospels represent Christian orthodoxy, then by definition they cannot be the bearers of the original truth. Leonardo and Mary speak from the margins and therefore speak truly, whereas Matthew, Mark, Luke, and John speak from a center fabricated by the imperial Roman church in the service of its own rise to power. Truth, it seems, is merely a matter of political location.

10. Ibid., 312–18.
11. Ibid., 333–34.
12. The question also arises in connection with the author's grasp of the geography of central London. If you wish to visit King's College London, you should take the underground *to*, not *from*, Temple underground station (see ibid., 483–84). In this connection, it is distressing that the name of the Research Institute in Systematic Theology—presided over by the late and much-loved Colin Gunton and by Christoph Schwöbel, at whose weekly seminars I myself took belated and faltering first steps in this discipline—should be misappropriated by the novelist to portray his crass vision of a high-tech religious database.

Images of the Son

Political factors may well have influenced the formation and imposition of the fourfold canonical gospel. Already in Ignatius, correlations are established between theological orthodoxy and episcopal control and between heterodoxy and independence. By the time of Irenaeus, these correlations have acquired a textual dimension: heterodoxy can now be associated with using the wrong texts or with failing to use the right ones. Yet the correlations are anything but straightforward. The heterodox may use the same canonical writings as their orthodox detractors, while interpreting them differently. Orthodoxy is itself an evolving and contested concept: bishops, like anyone else, may find themselves on different sides of an argument. The claim that there are four Gospels, no more and no less, is logically independent of issues such as episcopal authority or the role of women. In Ignatius, bishops preside over the church's worship; in Irenaeus, they uphold the rule of faith; but no one tries to legitimate episcopal authority by appealing to the fourfold gospel or to validate the fourfold gospel by deriving it from episcopal authority. And this means that the fourfold canonical gospel can be seen to pose a genuinely theological problem. Then as now, theology has its own integrity and should not be too quickly dismissed as a mere ideological smokescreen behind which one group seeks to impose its power over others.

The most significant attempt to justify the fourfold canonical gospel on theological grounds is the one offered by Irenaeus, which is of particular interest since it is (almost) as old as the fourfold gospel itself.[13] At its heart lies an image from Ezekiel 1

13. I pass over here the well-known account of the historical origins of the Gospels with which book 3 of *Against Heresies* opens (3.1.1). According to Martin Hengel, this passage is derived from historically valuable information that Irenaeus has obtained from "the Roman church archive"; *The Four Gospels and the One Gospel of Jesus Christ: An Investigation of the Collection and Origin of the Canonical Gospels* (trans. John Bowden; London: SCM, 2000), 37. Yet it seems likely that Irenaeus derived his information about Matthew and Mark from Papias (contra Hengel, 36). Irenaeus himself may have supplied the statement that Matthew wrote "when Peter and Paul were preaching the gospel in Rome" in order to establish Matthean priority: for Mark, "the disciple and interpreter of Peter," wrote in Rome "after their death." (In Papias, the references to Matthew and to Mark appear not to have been coordinated; see Eusebius, *Ecclesiastical*

as recycled in Revelation 4. In Ezekiel, the four mysterious figures who uphold the divine throne each have four faces: "And the likeness of their faces: the face of a human, and the face of a lion on the right for all four [*tois tessarsin*], and the face of a calf on the left for all four, and the face of an eagle for all four" (Ezek. 1:10 Septuagint, where the Greek translator renders Hebrew *šwr* ["ox"] as *moschos* ["calf"], a term with strong sacrificial connotations.) In Revelation, four figures again surround the divine throne, but each now has just one of the four faces: "And in the midst of the throne and around the throne [there were] four creatures [*zōa*], full of eyes before and behind. And the first creature was like a lion, and the second creature like a calf, and the third creature having a face as of a human, and the fourth creature like a flying eagle" (Rev. 4:6–7).

The traditional link between these four creatures and the four canonical Gospels derives from Irenaeus, who identifies the lion with John, the human with Matthew, the calf with Luke, and the eagle with Mark. Irenaeus attempts to show that the opening of each Gospel corresponds to these respective images (*Against Heresies* 3.11.8). Later versions of the scheme assign the eagle instead to John, which, according to Augustine, "soars like an eagle above the clouds of human infirmity" (*Harmony of the Gospels* 1.7). In Augustine's account, the first creature (the lion) is identified with the first evangelist (Matthew); the fourth creature (the eagle) with the fourth evangelist (John). The second and third evangelists change places, however: Augustine accepts Irenaeus's identification of the second creature (the calf) with Luke, the third evangelist, and the third creature (the human) with Mark, the second evangelist. Irenaeus's identifications of the creatures produce the order John, Luke, Matthew, and Mark—although he elsewhere shows that the order Matthew, Mark, Luke, and John was already familiar to him (*Against Heresies* 3.1.1).[14] In that sense, Augustine's revised order—Matthew, Luke, Mark, John—represents an improvement. Jerome takes the revision one step further by revert-

---

History 3.39.15–16.) The information of Papias and Irenaeus on gospel origins seems doubtful at every point. A purely historical argument for the fourfold gospel is no longer feasible: even the assumption that the canonical Gospels must predate the extant noncanonical ones is now open to question.

14. Later, however, the order is Matthew, Luke, Mark, and John, a reflection of Mark's inferior status; *Against Heresies* 3.9.1–11.7.

ing to Ezekiel, where the human face is in first rather than third place, yielding the order human, lion, calf, eagle (*Commentary on Matthew*, preface). The resulting equations exactly reproduce the traditional order of the Gospels: human = Matthew, lion = Mark, calf = Luke, eagle = John. It is these equations that have determined the artistic representation of the evangelists ever since.

As revised by Augustine and Jerome, Irenaeus's scheme is something of an imaginative triumph. The question is whether it has any theological substance. Certainly, the attempt to pair off each creature with each evangelist can hardly be taken seriously anymore. There is nothing obviously leonine about the Markan Jesus or calflike about the Lukan one. As for John and his eagle, "soar[ing] above the clouds of human infirmity" is exactly what the Johannine Jesus does *not* do. All four Gospels present a Jesus with a human face, and it is invidious to assign this to one evangelist rather than to another. If we are to make sense of Irenaeus's scheme, we must detach its theological substance from these one-to-one correspondences.

Why are there four Gospels, rather than one or many more? Irenaeus briefly suggests earthly analogies—four points of the compass, four winds, four pillars—but is much more interested in a heavenly one.[15] There is a fourfold gospel in the church because that is what the Lord gave us:

> The Word who is the maker of all things, who is seated upon the cherubim and holds all things together, in becoming manifest to humans, gave us the gospel in fourfold form [*edōken hēmin tetramorphon to euangelion*], held together by one Spirit—just as David says as he prays for his coming: "You who are seated upon the cherubim, manifest yourself [*emphanēthi*]!" (*Against Heresies* 3.11.8, citing Ps. 80:1 [= 79:2 in the Septuagint])[16]

The fourfold gospel is the gift of the Lord, integral to the self-manifestation to the world that occurs in his incarnation—the

15. As Eric Osborn points out, the earthly analogies show "how literally Irenaeus took the unity of creation and redemption"; *Irenaeus of Lyons* (Cambridge: Cambridge University Press, 2001), 175.

16. For the surviving Greek fragments of Irenaeus's third book, together with full Latin text, see *Irénée de Lyon: Contre les Hérésies* 3.2 (ed. A. Rousseau and L. Doutreleau; Sources chrétiennes 211; Paris: Cerf, 1974).

self-manifestation for which David prayed and which has now taken place, leaving behind the fourfold gospel as its permanent memorial. Why, though, does David associate the Lord with the cherubim? Why is the one whose incarnation he prays for addressed as the one "seated upon the cherubim"? And what has that to do with the fourfold gospel? Irenaeus knows the answer: "The cherubim," he tells us, "are four-faced [*tetraprosōpa*], and their faces are images of the mission of the Son of God [*eikones tēs pragmateias tou huiou tou theou*]" (*Against Heresies* 3.11.8). At this stage, the living creatures of Revelation 4 are seen as images of Christ himself, and not yet as images of the Gospels. But how can Irenaeus see "images of the mission of the Son of God" in these somewhat bizarre creatures? The answer is as follows:

> "And the first creature," [Scripture] says, "is like a lion"—thereby portraying [Christ's] active, ruling, and kingly qualities [*to emprakton autou kai hēgemonikon kai basilikon*]. "And the second was like a calf," disclosing his sacrificial and priestly ministry [*tēn hierourgikēn kai hieratikēn taxin*]. "And the third having the face [as if] of a man," outlining most clearly his coming as a human [*tēn kata anthrōpon autou parousian*]. "And the fourth was like a flying eagle"—revealing the gift of the Spirit hovering over the church. And so the gospels are consonant [*symphōna*] with these creatures among whom Christ is seated. (*Against Heresies* 3.11.8)

There is here a double analogy: an analogy within heaven itself, between Christ and the creatures, and an analogy that reaches from heaven to earth, from the four creatures as images or mirrors of Christ to the four Gospels acknowledged in the church.[17]

---

17. According to T. C. Skeat, there is a discrepancy between Irenaeus's appeals to Ps. 80:1, with its reference to the divine enthronement above the cherubim, and to Rev. 4, where the living creatures surround the divine throne, are not four-faced, and are not identified as cherubim; "Irenaeus and the Four-Gospel Canon," *Novum Testamentum* 34 (1992): 194–99, at 195. Also to be noted is the abrupt transition to the Revelation material (196). Skeat suggests that the gap in Irenaeus's argument can best be filled by postulating a source focused primarily on Ezek. 1 (198) (cf. Ezek. 10:20 for the identification with cherubim). If Irenaeus's identifications are read back into Ezek. 1, this would correspond to the so-called Western order of the Gospels (Matthew, John, Luke, and Mark), in place of the eccentric order that Irenaeus derives from Rev. 4 (John, Luke, Matthew, and Mark) (197–98). It is also possible, however, that Irenaeus himself is influenced by Ezek. 1 but has failed to mention it.

The creatures relate to Christ in heaven as the Gospels relate to Christ on earth; there is no direct identification of the creatures with the Gospels, but rather an analogy. The four creatures attest the four-dimensional mission of the Son of God: his regal authority, his sacrificial self-giving, his true humanity, and his bestowal of the Spirit. The four Gospels attest this same four-dimensional mission.[18]

Within the book of Revelation itself, the four creatures can plausibly be seen as images of the Son of God, just as Irenaeus claims. The first creature has a face like a lion, and Christ will shortly be announced as "the lion of the tribe of Judah," who has overcome and who is worthy to open the book sealed with seven seals (Rev. 5:4). The second creature has a face like a calf. There is no exact equivalence here, but the calf is a potential sacrificial victim, as Irenaeus rightly emphasizes, and when Christ, announced as the lion of Judah, actually appears, it is in the quite different form of a "Lamb standing as though slain" (5:6). The third creature has a human face. When Christ appears to John of Patmos, he does so as one "like a Son of Man, clothed with a long robe and with a golden girdle around his breast, his head and his hair white as white wool or as snow, his eyes as a flame of fire" (1:13–14). The fourth creature has a face like a flying eagle. Again, there is no exact equivalence, but Irenaeus's association of the eagle with the Spirit hovering over the church is influenced by the Christ of Revelation, who, as the Lamb standing as though slain, has seven horns and seven eyes, "which are the seven spirits of God sent into all the earth" (5:6). Christ is the conquering lion, the sacrificial victim, the glorified Son of Man, the bestower of the Spirit, and this Christ is mirrored in the four creatures with the faces of a lion, calf, human, and eagle. The analogy is not exact, but it cannot be discounted.

The Christ of Revelation seems constantly to change his appearance. Initially revealed as a human or superhuman figure, he is later announced as a lion but seen as a sacrificial Lamb whose horns and eyes speak of the outpoured Spirit. This Christ cannot be viewed all at once. He is not fully and absolutely himself in any one of these images. Rather, each image speaks of him under a

18. Elsewhere, Irenaeus tends to disparage analogies between the heavenly and the earthly; see Denis Minns, *Irenaeus* (London: Chapman, 1994), 26–28.

certain aspect and from a particular perspective. There is no single master-image, but rather an irreducible plurality. Yet, if we take the four living creatures as our guide, there is also no endless proliferation of images. As mirrored in the creatures around the throne, the Son of God has four main aspects. He is not a formless, protean being who can manifest himself as just about anything. The four living creatures mark out the space within which his identity is to be found, characterized as it is by regal power, self-sacrifice, true humanity, and the giving of the Spirit. In principle, there might have been a purely singular Christ mirrored in a single living creature and in a single definitive Gospel that placed him wholly within our grasp. Or there might have been an unlimited number of Christ images, in the form of heavenly creatures or earthly texts, richly diverse yet lacking all coherence. The four creatures and the four Gospels represent a *via media* between pure singularity and limitless plurality. They speak of a Christ who evades our attempts to grasp his being as a whole, yet whose person and work are subject to the constraints of definite form.

Understood in this light, Irenaeus's conclusion would seem to be warranted:

> As is the mission of the Son of God, such is the form of the creatures. And as is the form of the creatures, such is the character of the gospel. For the creatures are fourfold, the gospel is fourfold, and the mission of the Lord is fourfold. . . . Since this is so, all who disregard the appearance of the gospel [*tēn idean tou euangeliou*] are vain and still uninstructed and presumptuous, whether they promote more or fewer aspects of the gospels [*euangeliōn prosōpa*] than have been established here—the former so that they may seem to have found more of the truth, the latter so as to undermine the orderings of God [*tas oikonomias tou theou*]. (*Against Heresies* 3.11.8–9)

Subtracting from the four-dimensional gospel might seem to produce greater clarity, but would in fact impoverish our grasp of the infinite richness of the divine self-disclosure in Christ. Adding to the four-dimensional gospel might seem to reflect that infinite richness more adequately, but would in fact undermine its coherence. In principle, of course, there is no reason why five or six gospels should not have preserved the necessary coherence. The Pentateuch shows that there is nothing wrong with the number five; its creation account suggests no divine antipathy toward the number six. Yet Irenaeus is convinced that, in practice, supplementary gospels will quickly reveal their incompatibility with the four. For example, a text circulating among the Valentinians ambitiously titled *The Gospel of Truth*, "in nothing agreeing with the gospels of the apostles," ensures only that "there is with these people no gospel that is without blasphemy" (*Against Heresies* 3.11.9). Even the use of the canonical four is corrupted by the addition of this interloper.[19] Irenaeus has also heard of a *Gospel of Judas*, a product of a more extreme gnostic Christianity than the moderate, mildly intellectual Valentinian sort (1.31.1). This text depicted a power struggle between the God of Jewish Scripture and his mother Sophia, whose loyal followers—Cain, Esau, Judas himself—Scripture duly vilifies.[20] Exciting though this sounds, Irenaeus is surely right to conclude that confusion would reign were one to add Judas to Matthew, Mark, Luke, and John. There is no place for additional living creatures around the throne of God.

As we have seen, Irenaeus's attempt to correlate each creature with a particular evangelist is not a success. This was already clear in the ancient church, where there is consensus about only one of Irenaeus's analogies (Luke and the heavenly calf). Yet these analogies represent a remarkable acknowledgment and sanctioning of the *difference* between the Gospels. In themselves, the four living creatures are thoroughly heterogeneous, representing diverse orders of creation, united only in their praise of the one God, the Creator, and of the Lamb who was slain. This image actually serves to heighten the differences between the canonical Gospels, throwing them into the sharpest relief. As a result, Irenaeus finds himself advocating a form of relativism or perspectivism in which the reality transcends the individual text and yet is truly if partially

19. Irenaeus may here refer to a text known from Codex I and Codex XII from Nag Hammadi, which opens with the words: "The gospel of truth is a joy for those who have received from the Father of truth the gift of knowing him"; James M. Robinson, ed. *The Nag Hammadi Library in English* (San Francisco: Harper & Row, 1988), 38–51. As Koester points out, this text is "a homily or meditation" rather than "a writing that belongs to the gospel literature"; although the author knew and used written gospels, the term *gospel* still refers here to the message of salvation; *Ancient Christian Gospels*, 22–23.

20. It remains to be seen how far the recently published "Gospel of Judas" coincides with the text referred to by Irenaeus.

and provisionally attested in it. This relativism is at odds with the skeptical assumption that a truth-claim is undermined when its relativity is exposed. Truth may be partial, provisional, perspectival, inseparable from its limited textual embodiments, and yet still be truth—a finite expression of the all-comprehending, manifold yet singular truth of the divine self-disclosure in Jesus. In their fourfold canonical form, the Gospels relativize each other and at the same time affirm each other in their relativity. Rather than aspiring to lordship in their various domains, the four living creatures need one another if God and the Lamb are to be truly acknowledged and praised. A delicate dialectical balance is achieved between diversity and coherence—an alternative perhaps to the contemporary construal of difference and sameness as mutually exclusive opposites, each heavily fraught with social consequences for good or ill.

Gospels and Eucharist

The four living creatures take a leading role in the heavenly liturgy. They play the part of Isaiah's seraphim, calling out night and day, "Holy, holy, holy is the Lord God the Almighty, who was and who is and who is to come" (Rev. 4:8). They join with the twenty-four elders in singing a new song, a song of praise to the Lamb who was slain and who is worthy to open the book (5:8–10). They pronounce the "Amen" to a song of praise that finally encompasses every creature in heaven or on earth or under the earth or in the sea (5:13–14). They initiate and conclude the heavenly liturgy, standing in the midst of the worshiping congregation and articulating its praise of God and of the Lamb. The question is whether they have an earthly counterpart at this point too. Do the Gospels play a liturgical role within the church on earth as the living creatures do within the church in heaven? Irenaeus does not explicitly discuss this. Yet his older contemporary, Justin, goes some way toward making good this deficiency. Justin provides an unforgettably vivid depiction of the role of the Gospels within Christian eucharistic worship, and to this we now turn.[21]

---

21. For the Greek texts of Justin's writings, see E. J. Goodspeed, *Die ältesten Apologeten: Texte mit kurzen Einleitungen* (Göttingen: Vandenhoeck & Ruprecht, 1914).

At the close of his *First Apology*, written around 150 CE, Justin gives two parallel accounts of the Christian Eucharist as he knows it (*First Apology* 65; 67), separated by an important discussion of the rationale for this practice (66).[22] Between them, the two accounts provide an order of service with nine main elements. When the congregation is gathered together each Sunday, "the memoirs of the apostles or the writings of the prophets are read, for as long as there is time" (67.3). These "memoirs" are "called gospels" (66.3); that is, "memoirs" (*apomnēmoneumata*) is Justin's term for the texts generally known as "gospels." Following the reading is the homily, in which the president "gives instruction and exhortation to imitate these good things" (67.4). The Gospels are heard each Sunday, and the homily ensures that they serve to shape Christian praxis during the rest of the week as well. The homily is followed by intercession, in which "we offer heartfelt communal prayers for ourselves and . . . for all people in every place," that we and they together may finally attain salvation (65.1). The prayers completed, the worshipers greet one another with a kiss (65.2). Then bread and wine are brought to the president, the wine being mixed with water (65.3; 67.5), and the president gives thanks to the Father through the Son and the Holy Spirit that we are privileged to receive these precious gifts (65.3; 67.5). At the close of the thanksgiving, the worshipers express their assent by responding, "Amen" (65.3–5; 67.5), and those known as "deacons" (*diakonoi*) distribute the bread and wine to each worshiper in turn; it will also be distributed to those unable to attend the service (65.5; 67.5). Finally, a collection is taken for the support of needy members of the community (67.6).

As we shall see, the Gospels provide the rationale for the entire eucharistic rite, and, conversely, the Eucharist provides the coherent context for the gospel collection. First, however, we must ensure that we are still dealing with Matthew, Mark, Luke, and John. Unlike Irenaeus, Justin never explicitly claims that there are four Gospels, neither more nor less. Indeed, to judge from his citations, the Gospel of Matthew remains definitive for him,

22. While it is possible that the first account describes a special postbaptismal Eucharist, it is more likely that the two accounts refer to essentially the same rite. Justin is in the habit of repeating himself, as he himself acknowledges in *Dialogue with Trypho* 85.6; 118.4–5.

in its presentation both of the main narrative features of Jesus's life (birth, baptism, temptations, passion, resurrection) and of his teaching (the Sermon on the Mount is quoted extensively).[23] In second place is the Gospel of Luke, which Justin often draws on to supplement his Matthean narrative or teaching material. Here Luke's birth story begins to encroach on the Matthean one, especially in its account of the annunciation to Mary. Justin stands at the beginning of the process of harmonizing the Gospels.[24] His use of Luke's birth, passion, and resurrection narratives is motivated mainly by the search for further fulfillments of prophecy, in addition to those culled from Matthew (see *Dialogue with Trypho* 103.8; 105.5; 106.1). Not much use is made of Mark, although Justin knows this Gospel and can even refer to it as the "memoirs" of Peter (106.3, with reference to Mark 3:16–17). Yet Justin never explicitly refers to individual evangelists. Where he gives a source for his Gospel quotations, that source is usually "the memoirs of the apostles," "the memoirs of his apostles," or simply "the memoirs." The older tradition of speaking of "the gospel," thereby referring to Matthew, has largely disappeared (but cf. 100.1; 10.2). When Justin quotes from "the memoirs of the apostles," the cited passage represents not an individual evangelist but the entire collection.[25]

The place of the Gospel of John is ambiguous here. On the one hand, this Gospel is much less securely established in Justin than in Irenaeus, about thirty years later. Citations from John are almost as rare as they are from Mark (but see *First Apology* 61.4 [John 3:3, 5]; *Dialogue with Trypho* 88.7 [John 1:15, 20, 23]). On the other hand, Justin's theory of the Logos who becomes incarnate in Jesus seems massively indebted to the Johannine

23. See, for example, on Jesus's birth (*Dialogue with Trypho* 78.1–3, 7–8), baptism (49.3; contrast 88.7–8), temptations (103.6), passion (53.2; 101.3; 102.5), resurrection (108.1–2), and Sermon on the Mount (*First Apology* 15–16).

24. Harmonizing of the Lukan with the Matthean birth narrative is evident in *First Apology* 33.4–5; *Dialogue with Trypho* 78.4–5; and elsewhere.

25. At one point Justin speaks of "the memoirs composed by his apostles and those who followed him" (*Dialogue with Trypho* 103.8), which suggests that he knows at least four gospels; so G. N. Stanton, "The Fourfold Gospel," *New Testament Studies* 43 (1997): 317–46, at 330. Stanton argues that "we can be all but certain that he had in mind Matthew, Mark, Luke, and John, no more, no less" (331).

prologue, although this is never explicitly cited.[26] For example, Justin reflects on the term *monogenēs* ("only begotten"), which occurs twice in the Johannine prologue (John 1:14, 18). Christ was, Justin says, "the only begotten of the Father of all things, uniquely born from him as his Logos and Power, and later becoming human [*anthrōpos . . . genomenos*] through the virgin, as we have learned from the memoirs" (105.2). This indicates that the "memoirs" or Gospels teach not only that Christ was born of a virgin (Matthew, Luke) but also that this birth was the incarnation of the Logos who was the only begotten of the Father (John). Underlying Justin's *anthrōpos genomenos* is surely the *sarx egeneto* of John 1:14 (cf. *Second Apology* 6.3). Here and elsewhere, Justin harmonizes the Johannine incarnational Christology with the virginal conception tradition. In Luke's annunciation account, Mary is told that "the Holy Spirit will come upon you and the Power of the Most High will overshadow you" (Luke 1:35). Justin comments: "The Spirit and the Power that are from God are to be understood as none other than the Logos, who is the firstborn [*prōtotokos*] of God. . . . And this one, coming to the virgin and overshadowing her, caused her to conceive not through intercourse but through power" (*First Apology* 33.6). The Word became flesh at the moment when Mary was overshadowed by the Holy Spirit. This harmonizing of Johannine incarnational Christology with the Lukan virginal conception is fundamental to later Christian theological development and also serves to guarantee the Fourth Gospel a secure place in the canonical collection.[27] Justin stands at a crucially important moment in Johannine reception.

Each Sunday, the congregation hears the reading of "the memoirs of the apostles," commonly known as "gospels" (*First Apology* 67.3; 66.3). In an older liturgical tradition, it was "the gospel" that was read—that is, the Gospel of Matthew.[28] This remains the most

---

26. So M. Hengel: "Justin's Logos christology is inconceivable without the prologue of John"; *The Johannine Question* (London: SCM, 1989), 13.

27. This harmonizing was assisted—perhaps even occasioned—by the variant reading of John 1:13 as a reference to the virgin birth, certainly known to Irenaeus (*Against Heresies* 3.16.2; 3.19.2) and perhaps already to Justin. See also the *Epistula apostolorum* 3.

28. References to "the gospel" in the *Didache* (8.2; 11.3; 15.3–4) are probably to the Gospel of Matthew; contra Koester, *Ancient Christian Gospels*, 16–17.

prominent of the four, the one with which the congregation is most familiar. But it is now supplemented by readings from other Gospels: above all, from Luke, but also from Mark and John. In a sense, the four have coalesced into a single text, so that a passage is to be traced back not to an individual evangelist but to the Gospel collection as a whole. Christian worship, preaching, and thought is immeasurably enriched by the material the additional gospels make available. And it is the Eucharist, itself validated by the canonical Gospels, that guarantees that the coherence of Christian faith is preserved in spite of the plurality of texts. The fourfold gospel has a eucharistic context and rationale. It is in the Eucharist that the fourfold gospel is the singular entity that it is intended to be.

In the Eucharist, the Gospels are read, a homily is preached, prayers are offered, bread and wine are brought, thanksgiving is rendered, distribution is made. Why this focus on bread and wine? Justin answers:

> Not as ordinary food or ordinary drink do we receive these things. Rather, as through the word of God Jesus Christ our Savior was made flesh [*sarkopoiētheis*] and had flesh and blood for our salvation, so (we have been taught) the nourishment for which thanks are offered through the prayer of his word . . . is the flesh and blood of the Jesus who was made flesh. For the apostles, in the memoirs that come from them and are known as "gospels," record that they were instructed as follows: that Jesus, taking bread and giving thanks, said, "Do this in remembrance of me, this is my body." And likewise, taking the cup and giving thanks, he said, "This is my blood." And he imparted these things to them alone. (*First Apology* 66.2–3)

All four canonical Gospels are present in this crucially important passage; Justin's practice elsewhere may suggest that he (like Leonardo) is here consciously harmonizing the Gospel accounts. The command to "do this in remembrance of me" is drawn from Luke's eucharistic institution narrative (Luke 22:19).[29] Elsewhere Justin shows that he associates the Lukan *anamnēsis* or "remem-

29. On the originality of the longer text in Luke's eucharistic narrative, see Joseph A. Fitzmyer, *The Gospel according to Luke* (Anchor Bible 28–29A; New York: Doubleday, 1981–85), 1387–89; Bruce M. Metzger, *A Textual Commentary on the Greek New Testament* (New York: United Bible Societies, 1975), 173–77;

brance" specifically with Jesus's death, "that suffering [*pathos*] which the Son of God suffered for us" (*Dialogue with Trypho* 117.3; cf. also 41.1). Also Lukan are the phrase "taking bread [and] giving thanks"; the term *likewise*, which highlights the symmetry of Jesus's actions; and the definite article in the reference to "the cup" (Luke 22:19–20). However, the simplified words of institution—"this is my body," "this is my blood"—are dependent on Matthew and Mark, as are "taking [a] cup and giving thanks" and the concluding note about the apostles' participation (Matt. 26:26–28; Mark 14:22–24). Johannine influence is perceptible in the double reference to Jesus's "being made flesh" (cf. John 1:14) and in the association of his "flesh and blood" with the Eucharist (in contrast to the synoptic body and blood): "The one who eats my flesh and drinks my blood has eternal life" (6:54).[30] The incorporation of this Johannine perspective is highly significant, since it ensures that what is remembered in the Eucharist is not the death of Jesus considered in isolation, but his self-giving death as the goal of his incarnate life. It is, as it were, the whole Jesus who is imparted in the bread and wine, the Jesus of the full gospel narrative extending from incarnation to crucifixion and beyond. And it is the self-giving act of this Jesus, the Jesus of the fourfold canonical gospel, that is reenacted in every Eucharist.

We learned from Irenaeus to see the significance of the fourfold canonical gospel in its testimony to the plurality but also the concreteness of the truth embodied in Jesus. Like the living creatures, the gospel is *tetramorphon*, four-dimensional. Its plural perspectives on Jesus's identity cannot be reduced to one, as though the truth were susceptible to a single, definitive account, but neither can they be extended without limit, as though the truth were protean and formless. We have found that Justin has a somewhat different contribution to offer, one that has to do

---

and H. Schürmann, *Traditionsgeschichtliche Untersuchungen zu den synoptischen Evangelien* (Düsseldorf: Patmos, 1968), 159–97.

30. The Johannine flesh/blood terminology is probably influenced by the familiar pairing of "flesh and blood" in noneucharistic contexts (cf. Matt. 16:17; 1 Cor. 15:50; Gal. 1:16; Eph. 6:12; Heb. 2:14). For its application to the Eucharist, see also Ignatius, *To the Trallians* 8.1; *To the Romans* 7.3; *To the Philadelphians* 4.1; *To the Smyrnaeans* 7.1. There is no need to see this terminology as a vestige of the original Aramaic of the words of institution; contra J. Jeremias, *The Eucharistic Words of Jesus* (trans. Norman Perrin; London: SCM, 1966), 199.

with the social context that gives the canonical collection its rationale and coherence. That point of coherence is the Eucharist, celebrated each Sunday then as now.

For Justin as for others, the Christian Eucharist is the fulfillment of the prophecy of Malachi, that "from the rising of the sun to its setting my name is glorified among the nations, and in every place incense is offered to my name, and a pure sacrifice, so that my name is great among the nations—says the LORD Almighty" (Mal. 1:11).[31] According to Justin, the prophet speaks here of "the sacrifices offered in every place by us who are of the nations, that is, [the sacrifices] of the bread of the Eucharist and similarly of the cup of the Eucharist" (*Dialogue with Trypho* 41.3). As Justin's comment indicates, the Malachi text underlies the view of the Eucharist as a sacrificial rite in which an offering is made to God, to be received back from God as the life-giving means of salvation. The sacrificial action is not freestanding and autonomous, however. In this rite is reenacted the story of divine self-giving told by the fourfold gospel—the reenactment itself being authorized and commanded by the gospel. The reenactment secures our participation in the story and also serves to establish that it is indeed a single story that is told in the fourfold retelling. In a certain sense, the reenactment constitutes the story, providing it with its authoritative hermeneutic. Yet this is not the arbitrary imposition of a sense alien to the texts themselves, for, as Justin has helped us to see, it is the texts—all four of them—that validate the reenactment.

Where does this leave the noncanonical gospels? Clearly, they are not represented among the four living creatures who mirror the manifold truth of the Son of God. They have no heavenly counterparts. They do not belong to the gift bestowed by the Lord on the church to ensure that his once-for-all self-disclosure is perpetuated. They have no part to play in the Eucharist. Some of them, indeed, are ideologically opposed to the idea that the Lord took flesh and blood upon himself and gave himself as such in bread and wine. Such texts are the work of people who (as Ignatius of Antioch put it) "do not confess the Eucharist to be the flesh of our Savior Jesus Christ, who suffered for our

31. This passage is first applied to the Eucharist in *Didache* 14.3; see also Irenaeus, *Against Heresies* 4.17.5–6.

sins and was raised in the goodness of God" (*To the Smyrnaeans* 7.1). Apart from that, there is a great deal to be said for these texts. The world would be a poorer place without them. That they are detached from, or even opposed to, the liturgical life of the catholic church might be seen by some as a major point in their favor. No neutral criteria could determine that a Eucharist as described by Justin is the point of participation in the divine life, whereas the social context that produced, say, the *Gospel of Thomas* is not. The fourfold gospel may indeed have its own theological rationale—but theological rationales may be mistaken or outmoded and can never be proved to everyone's satisfaction.

Yet this patristic rationale for the fourfold gospel may still be of value to some—to those who continue to participate in the Eucharist, for reasons not unrelated to the ones Justin gives, and who continue to confess one, holy, catholic, and apostolic church in spite of compelling evidence that the church as we know it is none of those things. If four Gospels, neither more nor less, are still in use here, it is important to reflect on why this is the case—and important also to dispel the assumption that the church's practice must be arbitrary at best and untenable and discreditable at worst. In the face of such skepticism, we may continue to confess that the four Gospels have a heavenly origin, signified by the four living creatures, and an earthly destination, in the eucharistic life of the church. The four Gospels follow the course marked out by the divine Logos himself.

PART 2

RESPONSES

5

Authors, Readers, Hermeneutics

FRANCIS WATSON

The authors of this volume share a common concern to practice a theological exegesis. Since it is not immediately clear how one can or should go about such a practice, and since the very idea of a theological exegesis is controversial in some quarters, they also share a concern to reflect theoretically on what such a practice would involve. At the very least (they agree), exegesis must be put back into the church. It must be "ecclesial," ecclesially responsible exegesis. It must reckon with a context in which the scriptural texts are *not* read like other books, since issues of ultimate concern are uniquely and definitively articulated in them. For that reason, a line has been drawn around this collection of writings, demarcating it from other writings that may or may not perform analogous normative functions in other communities. And a rich tradition of interpretation has developed, in which one interpreter after another seeks to articulate those textually embodied issues of ultimate concern in ways accessible to his or her contemporaries. The authors of this volume are also agreed that the claims of modern biblical scholarship are to be resisted insofar as they prove incompatible with the claims of the ecclesial community, its canon, and its interpretive tradition. They are inclined to be skeptical of the familiar modernist rhetoric that proclaims the need to wrest the biblical texts from ecclesiastical control, to liberate them from the tyranny of dogma, to restore the original sense concealed by a long history of misreading. (Not that such a rhetoric does not sometimes have a point.) If these essays share a common ethos, the conveniently vague term *postliberal* might be as good a label as any.

My fellow authors are much exercised by the relation of author to reader—if we may take "author" as a figure for determinate sense, and "reader" as a figure for unlimited semiosis. Must readers learn to subject themselves to authors (human or divine), as Philemon must submit to Paul? Or do authors disappear from the scene, leaving behind them those sites of unlimited semantic abundance that we call "texts"? Are we to polemicize against the idea that we are "restricted . . . to a *single best option* for apprehending any given passage from the Bible" (see above, p. 21), that we should enforce "the *enclosure* of a realm of expression in which meaning's abundance can be confined to authorized, legitimized expressions" (see above, p. 18)? Or should we be more concerned at the prospect of libertarian readers so enamored of their readerly freedom that they manage to miss the great theodrama attested by the scriptural texts?

I am not sure that my modest defense of the fourfold canonical gospel can do much to resolve this conflict of hermeneutical priorities. As established in the late second century, *the fourfold gospel is the work of both authors and readers*. Naturally, the individual Gospels are the work of authors. According to Irenaeus, those authors were two apostles (Matthew and John) and two disciples of apostles (Mark and Luke). If Irenaeus was wrong about the names, his assumption of individual authorship was no doubt broadly correct. Yet things are not so simple. At least two of these authors were also readers. Matthew read Mark, Luke read Mark too and (in my opinion) also read Matthew. Unlike most readers, Matthew and Luke left behind a record of their reading, in the form of a new text that rewrote the older text(s). As anyone who has worked seriously with a Gospel synopsis will know, rewriting frequently entails a tacit critique of the earlier telling(s) of stories about Jesus. The later evangelist conceives it as his task to *improve on* the work of the earlier. Here, authors are readers, and readers are authors; authorial and readerly roles cannot be tidily demarcated. Reading seems to conform neither to the model of self-subjection to the prior canonical author nor to the model of unlimited semantic abundance. If these represent two ends of a readerly spectrum, then Matthew and Luke might be located somewhere in the middle. Their reading is free, but this freedom has its limits. And this relation to a prior text is typical of the entire phenomenon of biblical intertextuality, in which the constraint of the prior is a precondition of the freedom to differ and dissent.

Perhaps a greater interpretive liberty is bestowed on those readers who are also biblical authors than on those who are not? Conceivably, an interpretive license that would be improper for the rest of us might be sanctioned by divine inspiration (a claim often and unconvincingly used to explain the odder features of the New Testament's use of the Old). But, if the fourfold gospel is at all indicative, the author/reader relationship continues to be anything but straightforward, even after the canonical authors have laid down their pens. It is plausible to suppose that Matthew understands himself as the author of an enlarged, improved second edition of Mark. Similarly, Luke's prologue suggests—without quite saying so—that his own careful research makes his Gospel more dependable than his predecessors. The Gospel of John claims to derive from an anonymous disciple uniquely close to Jesus and so possessed of superior insight into his person and significance. Each subsequent Gospel seeks to improve on its predecessor(s); each makes a bid for definitive status. With the arrival of Matthew (it might have been thought), Mark will no longer be needed. When Marcion preferred Luke to the others, he may have correctly divined the evangelist's intention. *And yet*, it is for readers, not authors, to decide what to read and how it will be read. It seems that the majority of early readers chose not to choose between Matthew or Mark or Luke or John, but preferred to choose all four. They thereby took it upon themselves to address the inevitable problem of coordinating the divergent narratives, an interpretive challenge that issued in Justin's harmonizing, in Irenaeus's spectacular venture into

metaphorical theology, and in Origen's courageous subordination
of historical truth to theological truth. The problem arose out of
decisions made *both* by authors (who were themselves readers)
and by subsequent readers (who were themselves redactors of
the new, quadriform text).

If this case study in authorial/readerly relations has any wider
implications, it may suggest that no one-sided subjection of
readers to authors, or of authors to readers, will be adequate for
the complexities of a given interpretive situation—at least where
it is a genuinely *theological* interpretation that is at stake.

Perhaps our hermeneutics needs to be more comprehensive.
We may need to expand our hermeneutical repertoire. In the
one classic hermeneutical treatise of the Christian tradition,
On Christian Doctrine, Augustine argued that the theological
interpreter should be equipped with the following items:

1. A firm grasp of the *telos* of Holy Scripture and its interpretation, which is to engender the love of the Triune God
   and of the neighbor and nothing else.
2. A personal orientation toward holiness and the fear of
   God.
3. An ability to reach an informed decision about the precise
   scope of the scriptural canon.
4. An intimate familiarity with the entire Bible.
5. A knowledge of Hebrew and Greek, to facilitate clearer
   understanding of authorial intention.
6. An expertise in textual criticism, so as to eliminate cor-
   ruptions of the text.
7. A broad acquaintance with secular sciences, especially
   history and logic.
8. An ability to identify and decide between competing exegetical possibilities.
9. An awareness of the differences between current social
   conventions and those of the biblical past.
10. An understanding of scriptural tropes and rhetoric.
11. A sense of the manifold interpretive possibilities of the
    biblical text—possibilities intended by the author and/or
    Holy Spirit, in token of the divine abundance.

Strikingly, Augustine at no point suggests that these items are in competition with one another. For example, he does not argue that an expertise in textual criticism, while all very well in its way, pales into insignificance in comparison with the fear of the Lord, which is the beginning of wisdom. He does not suggest that secular or technical aspects of biblical interpretation may safely be overlooked by those who seek (and rightly so!) only the text's spiritual sense. Needless to say, it does not occur to Augustine that professing Christians might wish to abstract the secular and technical aspects of interpretation from their over-arching context in the spiritual formation of the individual and community. Augustine everywhere assumes that texts embody an author's communicative intentions and that it is the task of interpretation to clarify these. Yet this in no way inhibits the semantic abundance intended and disclosed by the Holy Spirit, beyond what was consciously intended by the human author.

The authors of the present book might wish to put some of these points differently or add new ones. Yet I suspect that none of us would dissent significantly from Augustine's comprehensive program for the renewal of theological exegesis. And perhaps Augustine challenges us to consider whether we may have been a little too eager to pit one interpretive priority against others, as though they were mutually exclusive.

6

Further Thoughts
on Theological Interpretation

STEPHEN E. FOWL

In this limited response to the well-crafted essays of my colleagues, I aim to do two things. First, I will try to situate my
essay within the scope of my larger concerns with theological
interpretation of Scripture. Then, I will take up the particular
and very provocative images of freedom and slavery that Kevin
Vanhoozer raises in his essay. I do not pick this issue because it
is badly done; quite the opposite. Thinking about interpretation
in this way, however, will help to clarify some of the differences
that may remain between us, despite the large amount of area
in which we agree.

Although much of my graduate training and early scholarly
writings were concerned with issues of philosophical hermeneutics, I no longer think these are the primary issues for interpreting
Scripture theologically. In short, I no longer think that a general
theory of textual meaning is crucial to interpreting Scripture theo-

logically. If one's exegetical practice is governed by some sort of general hermeneutical theory, then it is very hard to avoid the situation where theological interpretation of Scripture becomes the activity of applying theological concerns to exegesis done on other, nontheological grounds. One of the points I have tried to argue persistently over the past several years is that the key to interpreting theologically lies in keeping theological concerns primary to all others. In this way, theology becomes a form of exegesis, not its result.[1] Thomas Aquinas and other premodern interpreters do this better than most scholars today. This is not to say that we should follow all of Thomas's or Luther's or Chrysostom's exegetical conclusions. Rather, what premodern interpreters can display for our edification is the importance of making sure that theological concerns regulate the literal sense of Scripture. When we fail to do that, when we let historical or sociological or some other set of concerns regulate scriptural interpretation, for example, it is hard to avoid the conclusion that trinitarian dogma provides a very clumsy and unpersuasive way of reading John 1. Unless theological concerns are primary, then christological readings of Isaiah can seem to be only secondary, parasitic interpretations, rather than the literal sense of those texts.

Instead of relying on a hermeneutical theory to provide the *telos* of theological interpretation of Scripture, Christians must remember that they are called to interpret and embody Scripture as a way of advancing toward their true end of ever deeper love of God and neighbor. Scripture is chief among God's providentially offered vehicles that will bring us to our true home. This vehicle can seem so plush and its ride so smooth that we can forget that we are on a journey and end up loving the ride more than we desire to get to the end of the journey. To resist that temptation, Christians need to make sure that our interpretations and embodiments of Scripture are always directed toward enhancing our prospects of reaching our true home.[2]

This focus, along with the notion that the Spirit as the author of Scripture ensures a multiplicity of meanings within the literal

1. To see this distinction displayed a bit more fully, see the introduction to Stephen E. Fowl, *Philippians* (Two Horizons New Testament Commentary; Grand Rapids: Eerdmans, 2005).
2. This is one of Augustine's persistent themes in book 1 of *On Christian Doctrine* (trans. D. W. Robertson; New York: Macmillan, 1958).

sense of Scripture, however, raises the specter of interpretive anarchy in which any and all interpretations become acceptable. One can detect this concern behind the drive to provide some sort of hermeneutical regulation for scriptural interpretation. One might even go so far as to point to the extreme cases of *The Da Vinci Code* or *The Prayer of Jabez* as the most recent examples of what might happen when one leaves Scripture unguarded by a secure hermeneutic.

As I argue in various places and ways, keeping theological concerns primary in scriptural interpretation places the burden of regulating and adjudicating specific scriptural interpretations and interpretive disputes within an ecclesial context.[3] Christian communities, local congregations, should be the places where Christians are formed through word and sacrament to read Scripture in the light of their proper ends in Christ. The church is the place where they are to be formed—through catechesis, worship, and prayer—to understand what their proper ends in Christ are; the place where, in the course of forming a common life worthy of the gospel of Christ (cf. Phil. 1:27), they learn the conversational habits and practices to enable them to argue over Scripture in ways that enhance their prospects of moving toward their proper ends in Christ.[4]

In this light, it is interesting that two of the essays explicitly mention the extraordinary popularity and influence of *The Da Vinci Code*. I can also testify to the influence of this work on my own students. I would argue, however, that the influence of such a ridiculous and implausible account is not the result of a failure of hermeneutics, but a failure of catechesis.

In trying to think through the implications both of my argument here about Thomas and of the larger set of arguments I have been making about theological interpretation, it seems clear to me that I have much more work to do in exploring the relationships between ecclesiology and scriptural interpretation. I am particularly concerned with trying to figure out what place this theologically regulated, ecclesially located form of scriptural interpretation has in a fractured church.

3. See Stephen E. Fowl, *Engaging Scripture: A Model for Theological Interpretation* (Oxford: Blackwell, 1998), chap. 3.

4. I take it that this is also the response that A. K. M. Adam offers to those who fear interpretive anarchy.

My thinking here is quite preliminary, but I would like to offer two brief points in this regard. First, Scripture and debates about scriptural interpretation are not the cause of church division in any sort of direct way. Long before the Reformation, Christians engaged in rather sharp and substantial disagreements with one another over scriptural interpretation without tearing the body of Christ apart. Look at the letters between Augustine and Jerome or Theodore of Mopsuestia's account of Origen to name just two famous examples. Rather, when the church divides over Scripture, it is not so much an issue of scriptural interpretation as it is the result of a separation of scriptural interpretation from a variety of other ecclesial practices. These practices are held together by love, by the love that Christ has for believers and that Christ commands believers to have for one another. All church division is fundamentally a failure of love. All division proceeds from believers assuming that they are better off apart from one another than together. Division is a contradiction of ecclesial love, especially our love of our enemies within Christ's body. Differences of scriptural interpretation cannot divide the church unless there is a prior failure of love.

Second, Scripture does not directly address church divisions in the ways that we currently know them. The New Testament does not, perhaps cannot, imagine Christ's body fractured in the ways it has been for almost five hundred years. Hence, there is no point in plumbing Scripture's depths in order to see what Scripture "says" about church division. Instead, I would argue that scriptural accounts about Israel's division (e.g., Jer. 3; Ezek. 39; Ps. 106; Isa. 6:10; 28:9; 29:9–13) and New Testament texts such as Romans 9–11 and Ephesians 2–3 can help us begin to develop a scripturally shaped language and sets of categories for talking about these divisions in the present and how to understand the consequences of division.[5]

Thus far, I have tried to fit my essay into a larger trajectory of my prior work and to indicate some future directions and issues for theological interpretation of Scripture. At this point I would like to respond to Vanhoozer's essay and its emphasis on

5. Although I do not always read these texts as he does, my views here rely heavily on Ephraim Radner, *The End of the Church* (Grand Rapids: Eerdmans, 1998).

the master/slave image. I found Vanhoozer's essay very engaging and filled with typically rigorous and self-reflective insight. My aim here is primarily to set out a question that stuck with me after reading the essay.

To begin, I want to return briefly to Augustine's *On Christian Doctrine*, to which I made allusion earlier. Augustine's discussion and concerns about enjoying the ride so much that one forgets about arriving at one's destination is one example of his more general concern in book 1 of *On Christian Doctrine*, namely, that Christians need to order their relationships with their surroundings in such a way as to love the right things in the right way so that ultimately their love is directed properly to God.

In terms of my own views on theological interpretation, I have always felt that Vanhoozer's work offers one of the strongest and most sophisticated alternatives.[6] It is with this in mind that I want to explore the master/servant image that energizes much of Vanhoozer's essay. When Vanhoozer argues that theological hermeneutics is primarily about determining the appropriate status of author, text, subject matter, and community relative to each other, I recognize this as a long-standing emphasis in his work. I was, thus, surprised when Vanhoozer later says: "Theological hermeneutics is a matter, first, of grasping the basic plot— of being able to relate the various scenes in the theodrama to what God has done climactically in Jesus Christ and, second, of grasping how we can go on following Christ in new situations so that our speech and action corresponds to the truth of the gospel" (see above, p. 77). At this point, I am very much in agreement with him.

In this later comment, Vanhoozer's first point emphasizes that Christians must regulate their interpretation of Scripture theologically in the light of something like the rule of faith. However one might want to fine-tune the contours of the rule of faith, it basically provides the dramatic framework for appropriately ordering the diversity of Scripture. This recognition goes back at least as far as Irenaeus. Vanhoozer's second point emphasizes the importance of Christ-focused practical reasoning so that

6. See especially Kevin J. Vanhoozer, *Is There a Meaning in This Text? The Bible, the Reader, and the Morality of Literary Knowledge* (Grand Rapids: Zondervan, 1998).

Christians can interpret Scripture in the light of the various circumstances in which they find themselves in ways that will enhance their deepening communion with God. The criterion for evaluation of interpretive performance is its fittingness (a deeply Thomistic notion!). Determinations of fittingness are the result of the proper display of cruciform wisdom.

In the light of this, it appears that our two positions are very close. Given what Vanhoozer has said thus far, it seems to me that there is a relatively straightforward way to proceed with his initial set of concerns over authors, texts, status, and freedom. This way would say that these are not and should not be the central concerns of theological interpretation. The different aims and purposes that Christians bring to theological interpretation raise different sets of questions that do not really bear on the philosophical concerns of authors, readers, and texts. Should these concerns need to be adjudicated with regard to a particular text in a specific setting, this can be done in an ad hoc way. This is why interpreters such as Augustine and Thomas are quite relaxed about what one can attribute to the human authors of Scripture.

In terms of masters and servants, submission to texts and their human authors seems relatively subsidiary to submission to God. Indeed, given Augustine's concerns, too strong an emphasis on submission to Scripture or Scripture's human authors seems to hold the real possibility of misdirecting one's attention from reaching one's true home.

I do not mean to draw an impenetrable barrier between philosophy and theology. Rather, given the concern to read Scripture in the light of the rule of faith and with cruciform wisdom, the connections to philosophical and hermeneutic concerns with authors, texts, communities, and so forth seem remote. As it now appears that Vanhoozer's current views and my views seem so similar, I would like to know further from him how these current views require his earlier philosophical concerns with authors, texts, and readers. One option might be to say that to the extent that the concerns of philosophical hermeneutics impinge on Vanhoozer's theodramatic approach, they would appear to be much more in line with those of A. K. M. Adam's essay. That, however, would be to presume an answer to a question I genuinely offer here as part of an ongoing conversation rather than the last word on anything.

7

Four Theological Faces of Biblical Interpretation

KEVIN J. VANHOOZER

If these essays are indicative of recent trends, then the "iron curtain" that has separated the church from the academy and biblical studies from dogmatics has turned into something altogether more gossamerlike: exegetes and systematicians can now see and hear one another, albeit at times rather hazily. I cannot help but think that text, church, academy, and world alike will benefit from the end of this hermeneutical cold war.

Each of my colleagues strives in his own way to advance the cause of the theological interpretation of Scripture on biblical hermeneutics' western front. I have learned much from each and count them all as strategic allies in the attempt to free the Bible from its recent captivity in the cold ivory towers of academia. What differences there are emerge out of a common concern to do justice to the plurality found in Scripture and tradition while recognizing that not every interpretation is legitimate. All four of us want to say that a *little* plurality need not be a dangerous thing, yet we diverge in our attempts to explain how such plurality can be delimited and principled rather than merely infinite and arbitrary. I want to highlight our similarities and differences by considering our respective accounts of what we may call *prolific* hermeneutics, yet another variation on the ancient problem of "the one and the many."

For Plurality?

"But there are also many other things which Jesus did; were every one of them to be written, I suppose that the world itself could not contain the books that would be written" (John 21:25). Clearly, there is ample biblical warrant to rejoice in textual abundance. The life of the Word made flesh is prolific, giving birth to multiple gospels, commentaries, and christologies. Yet it is absurd to think that every interpretation that purports to be a faithful representation of the history of Jesus and its significance is so. "Be fruitful and multiply" (Gen. 1:28) is hardly a mandate for hermeneutical license; one cannot simply equate the sheer multiplication of meaning with fruitfulness.

"You will know them by their fruits" (Matt. 7:16). Fruitfulness means more than producing multiple meanings and interpretations. My colleagues are prolific scholars in the sense that they are abundantly productive. But should we be prolific in the sense of producing many offspring? Is not that function—the begetting of meaning—the role of the author? Jesus himself seemed to think that it was possible for interpreters to get it wrong: "You search the scriptures, because you think that in them you have eternal life; and it is they that bear witness to me" (John 5:39).

Just as Jesus's disciples were accountable to that "which we have looked upon and touched with our hands, concerning the word of life" (1 John 1:1), so interpreters are accountable to that which we have heard, seen, and touched in Scripture. If the vocation of the interpreter is to be a witness to the authorial discourse on christological matter, then it follows that the interpreter-witness, like the biblical authors themselves, is necessarily bound to what has already been said and done. If I profess and practice determinate interpretation, then, it is not because of some general hermeneutical theory but because I believe that the ultimate purpose of Scripture is to witness to what God has done in Jesus Christ. Determinacy is a function of the specific content of the Gospel; if the interpreter-witness is not able to exhaust the meaning of divine discourse, it is not because it is unstable or indeterminate, but because "the world itself could not contain the books that would be written." Theological interpretation, then, is ultimately a martyrological act.

It need not follow that there is no room for creativity or even improvisation, to use a term from my own essay above.[1] The phrase *prolific hermeneutics* states our common concern: how to affirm the fruitfulness and goodness of textual and interpretive polyphony without discrediting the integrity and specificity of the canonical witness to Jesus Christ. The devil, or at least his adjuncts, is in the details, hence the temptation to demonize those who may not parse polyphony the way we do.

Against Theory?

All four of us acknowledge not only a certain plurality of texts and readings but also certain parameters to our respective interpretive practices. Nevertheless, I detect a pronounced anti-theoretical bias on the part of my three dialogue partners, each of whom makes a special point of *not* subscribing to a "theory" of interpretation.

To paraphrase Jesus: "The pragmatist you shall always have with you." My colleagues display a number of telltale symptoms of contemporary theory-phobia: a reluctance to employ key terms like "meaning" or "truth" with capital letters; an inclination to begin with practice, not reflection; an avoidance of too close a tie to any one interpretive method or hermeneutical program; an openness to the many activities that pass for interpretation. Perhaps they might argue that the polyphonic matter of Scripture requires a plurality of methods and approaches. I have a good

1. In Kevin J. Vanhoozer, *Is There a Meaning in This Text? The Bible, the Reader, and the Morality of Literary Knowledge* (Grand Rapids: Zondervan, 1998), two kinds of interpretive freedom are examined: a carnivalesque freedom *from* and a covenantal freedom *for* (434–38).

deal of sympathy for such a view; I certainly make no claim to possess for myself the One True Approach to the One True Meaning of Scripture. At the same time, I am uneasy when hermeneutic pragmatists no longer care about "getting it right." Love and justice—with regard to the discourse and to the matter in question—serve as regulative ideals for theological hermeneutics too, even if our interpretations never fully exhaust them.

It was Jesus himself who taught his disciples how to interpret Israel's Scriptures theologically. Faith's search for understanding must therefore begin with an apprenticeship to Jesus's own reading practice. Theological hermeneutics is ultimately a matter of unpacking the logic not of ecclesial but of dominical interpretive practices.[2] Theological hermeneutics can be theoretical, then, if by theoretical we mean giving some explanation or account of why we read the way we do.

Watson: The Calf

The four creatures mentioned in Francis Watson's essay present a metaphor with which to describe the present collection of essays that is too good to ignore. Not only are there four authors, but each of us has four faces in the sense that we look in the direction of our own agendas but also turn to dialogue with the other three. I had no problem assigning to each of us a specific face. Watson, with his emphasis on Jesus's passion and its eucharistic rehearsal as the proper context for biblical interpretation, is the calf. Stephen Fowl, with his emphasis on reading in the ecclesial communion created by the Holy Spirit is (appropriately enough) the eagle. A. K. M. Adam is (obviously) the human, not only because he bears the name of the first man but also because he practices "only human" interpretation, from below. I reluctantly take on the last face myself, not least because I see my early work in particular as Barth did his ("well roared, lion").

Watson is rightly appreciative of the polyphonic nature of the Gospels' identity narratives. He is equally aware of the exclusion-

---

2. Kevin J. Vanhoozer, *The Drama of Doctrine* (Louisville: Westminster/ John Knox, 2005) argues for locating authority in "canonical practices"—the commissioned discourse of the prophets and apostles that serve as a creaturely medium for divine authority.

ary nature of the distinction between canonical and noncanonical attempts to identify Jesus. Not just any voice is authorized to name Jesus Christ: "If replaced by other texts, the outcome would be not only another Jesus but also another community" (see above, p. 96). He draws the correct inference from this situation: there must be something *determinate* about what these texts say about Jesus, or else one set of texts would do as well as another.

The challenge is to defuse the *Da Vinci Code*–like suspicion that the canonical boundaries are arbitrary or, worse, motivated politically by a lust for ecclesial power. Watson's creative retrieval of the image of the four four-faced creatures from Ezekiel 1 as recycled in Revelation 4 and recapitulated by Irenaeus makes for fascinating reading. The basic idea is that the four creatures, and hence the four Gospels, attest the four-dimensional mission of the Son. Watson infers that the reality of Jesus Christ is too rich to be captured by any one narrative or, we could add, by any one conceptual or doctrinal scheme. The four creatures and the four Gospels represent "a *via media* between pure singularity and limitless plurality" (see above, p. 107).

Watson is absolutely right to call our attention to the "plural unity" of the Gospels' attestation of Jesus as the Christ and to the partial yet genuine nature of their textually mediated truth. The discourse of the New Testament is polyphonic, and premature systematizations wreak violence on the texts. I also agree that the Gospels are used not only to identify Jesus Christ but also to draw us into his life by soliciting our participation in the Eucharist, a concrete realization of fellowship with God and with one another. If I have understood Watson aright, the argument is not that eucharistic practice provides an external justification for the four Gospels, but rather that such practice is both context and consequence for understanding the fourfold gospel. Putting Watson's point in my own terms: the Eucharist is a command performance of the church's script and hence a paradigmatic *canonical* practice.

Fowl: The Eagle

Where Watson sees theological interpretation of Scripture as a matter of using the text to think with, Fowl argues that the primary aim of theological interpreters ought to be using the text to *worship* with. In his important 1998 work *Engaging Scripture*, he contrasts determinate and antideterminate interpretation, only to dismiss them both in favor of an underdetermined interpretation that avoids appealing to some theory of meaning to guide interpretation. Whereas determinate interpretation "views the biblical text as a problem to be mastered," antideterminate interpretation aims "to upset, disrupt, and deconstruct interpretive certainties."[3] As to underdetermined interpretation, it "recognizes a plurality of interpretive practices and results without necessarily granting epistemological priority to any one of these."[4]

The main thrust of Fowl's essay is to argue that the literal sense of Scripture is itself polyphonic and hence underdetermined because, according to Thomas Aquinas, the divine author intends many meanings. This seems to be a significant convergence with my own emphasis on divine authorial discourse. I agree that the literal sense need not be single; authors can do several things at once with their words on different levels.[5] I am less sanguine about Fowl's retooled literal sense, however, when it begins to work against the stability and sufficiency of Scripture as a basis for theology.

Let me pose two questions. First, how should we describe the polyphony that both Fowl and I affirm in Scripture? I am struck by the semantic slippage that occurs in Fowl's essay. The title affirms a "multivoiced" literal sense, but the text itself alternates between speaking of (1) a "multifaceted" literal sense, (2) many manifestations of the literal sense, and (3) many literal senses. My own solution is to affirm a single, though complex, literal sense and then to give a thick description of its manifold aspects. By contrast, Fowl's inclination is to affirm a plurality of literal senses for the same passage. I fear that it is a non sequitur to conclude that there may be many literal senses just because the Spirit speaks more than humans can comprehend.

3. Stephen E. Fowl, *Engaging Scripture: A Model for Theological Interpretation* (Oxford: Blackwell, 1998), 32.
4. Ibid., 10.
5. My own essay calls for an abandoning of the literal-figurative distinction in favor of a deflationary account that simply describes what authors, human and divine, are doing with their words (see p. 71 above).

And this leads to my second question. Fowl is in favor of many (but not too many!) legitimate interpretations. Yet throughout his essay, he makes a special point of saying that Thomas has no problem ruling out some interpretations to be inadequate or mistaken. How can we delimit what God intends to be understood by the words that are written? The general idea is that, instead of delimiting, we should rather accept as many true meanings as possible. There is, however, an important caveat: "Do not violate the context."

Fowl examines Thomas's suggestion that "in the beginning was the Word" (John 1:1) has (at least) three literal meanings and asks whether Thomas was "right." Specifying criteria for interpreters "getting it right" is, in my book, what hermeneutical theory is all about. So, does Fowl succeed both in establishing many literal senses and in providing a criterion that halts their endless proliferation? Readers will have to judge for themselves. Let me call attention to one interesting fact. Thomas derives his three interpretations of John 1:1 on the basis of the various ways of using the term *principium*. But this is a Latin term, and the author of the Fourth Gospel wrote in *Greek*.

"Determinate" means limited in time and space. Is it not a violation of the context of John 1:1 to lift the text from its original time and place, not to mention its original language? There is a christological point here that should not be missed. God makes himself known and communicates to humans not by transcending space and time but by entering into the human condition. To divorce Scripture from its historical context is to suggest that it has the mere *appearance* of human discourse. This way lies hermeneutic Docetism. In order not to violate the text, must we not eventually say that the eagle has landed in some determinate time and place?

Fowl is right to insist that the divine intention ultimately transcends that of the human author. I argue in my own essay that theological hermeneutics is a matter of "discerning the divine discourse in the work." Where we still differ, perhaps, is in the way that we respond to the injunction not to violate the context. For me, context refers to the historical, literary, and canonical settings of biblical discourse. It is not entirely clear to me how Fowl would appeal to context—which contexts?—in order to delimit the plurality of possible divine intentions.

Adam: The Human

It falls to Adam to make the most explicit case on behalf of not only a prolific but also a proliferating hermeneutics, and he does so by contrasting it with what he takes to be the mainstream, "integral" tendency in biblical interpretation that aims at "getting it right."[6] Adam worries that the very notion of "getting it right" implies that others, who do not do what we do, will get it wrong. This leads to "polemics and exclusion"—to the minimalizing of meaning and the marginalizing of readers. In presenting the situation in this way, however, Adam creates yet *another* divisive polarity, namely, a distinction between integral polarizers and differential nonpolarizers. But has there not always been a certain polarization between God's people and "not-my-people"? In the pre-Reformation church, the polarities were orthodoxy and heresy. We find similar polarizations within Scripture itself: light and dark, true and false, life and death.

I understand Adam's hermeneutic claustrophobia; I do not want to restrict myself to a single exegetical method either. Methods are simply formalizations of certain insights into the nature of textual discourse; there may be many insights into what the human and divine authors are doing in a given text. I therefore read to discover *all* that the human and divine authors do in using just these words in just these ways. This yields not a specific method so much as a regulative goal. If I insist on "getting it right," it is not because I am a hermeneutical monist who believes that texts have but one meaning (much less that I have it!) but because I believe in the integrity (i.e., oneness, wholeness, entirety) of the gospel.

Adam's "differential" hermeneutics shifts attention away from readers' ethical obligation to authors and toward their ethical obligation to other readers. The image of the human face here comes into its own: the philosopher Levinas argues that we

6. "Integral" is the label that Adam uses in a previous publication in which he also interacts with Fowl, Watson, and me. In that essay he identifies his own position as "differential" hermeneutics; see A. K. M. Adam, "Integral and Differential Hermeneutics," in *The Meanings We Choose: Hermeneutical Ethics, Indeterminacy, and the Conflict of Interpretations* (ed. Charles H. Cosgrove; Journal for the Study of the Old Testament Supplement 411; Edinburgh: T&T Clark, 2004), 24–38.

cannot "theorize" about faces because each face is unique and singular.[7] Ethics is a matter of respecting this otherness: "Thou shalt not kill." The question, however, is whether one can respect others without also respecting authors. What is theological interpretation if it is not a matter of bearing witness to what God has said through human authors? Adam needs to say more about what I called the status relations that obtain between authors, texts, and readers.

The core of Adam's argument is his apology for a prochoice hermeneutics and the concomitant proliferation of interpretation.[8] What keeps proliferating hermeneutics from becoming profligate? The problem is not the sheer plurality of interpretations—plurality is a sign of abundance—but the possibility of interpretations that misrepresent Jesus and, we might add, the possibility of interpretations that misrepresent God and the gospel. How do we keep from doing that? Adam maintains that the church has always had "local" criteria based on the convergence of two or more interpreters' shared sense of which aspects of the text count. But Adam does not extrapolate from the local to the global; he does not believe that there is a universal set of norms for distinguishing valid from invalid interpretations because, as we have seen, this implies interpretive conflict over who is correct. The unity by which believers profess their allegiance to the one God is not the unity of truth but the unity of tolerance, "the obligation to bear with one another."[9]

To care about catholicity is to attend to how the whole church in its extension in time and space reads Scripture. Here we might ask whether Adam adequately qualifies his profligate understanding of unity and catholicity with the other marks of the church: holy, apostolic. Unity and catholicity work as criteria only if there is an agreement as to who "we" are. I doubt that Adam's inclusivity extends as far as Arians, Deists, or Scientologists. But why not? Do not they have local criteria too? The limits of Adam's interpretive profligacy, and his final word on criteria, are a function not of hermeneutics but of Christology: Christians must

7. Emmanuel Levinas, *Totality and Infinity: An Essay on Exteriority* (Pittsburgh: Duquesne University Press, 1969), 50, 295.

8. The title of the book in which this earlier essay appears is *The Meanings We Choose*.

9. Adam, "Integral and Differential Hermeneutics," 38.

exclude interpretations that misrepresent Jesus. Adam invokes what he calls "a physiognomy of legitimate interpretation"[10] for which the only thing that matters is the face of God in Christ and getting *that* right. But we can only judge misrepresentations of Jesus, I contend, over against an authoritative, and determinate, biblical template. Such is precisely what we have in the prophetic and apostolic discourse set aside by the Spirit in the canon with the express aim of presenting Christ.

Concluding Unleonine Postscript

All four of us acknowledge a legitimate polyphonic presence in theological interpretation: a plurality of canonical Gospels (Watson), literal senses (Fowl), signifying practices (Adam), scripted performances (Vanhoozer). All of us, similarly, acknowledge certain limitations to this plurality. We differ, however, in our accounts of the nature of this plurality and in our attempts to circumscribe it.

I have ascribed to myself the face of the lion. Yet, if the truth be told, the face of my theological hermeneutics better resembles that of the lowly ass: it is a humble proposal for hearing the biblical word, itself a creaturely medium for bearing the Word born to be king. What I have set forth here is not a Grand Old Theory to lord hermeneutically over others but a modest account of what I take to be best interpretive practice.

My theory does not give any particular interpreter or interpretive community favored status. Like the Reformers, I regard my own readings as provisional, open to correction by others who may see more clearly into the text than do I. The voice to which I want to ascribe authority is not my own, but rather the voices of Jesus Christ and the Holy Spirit speaking in and through the commissioned human authors of the Bible who tell us, with pregnant determinacy, what God is doing in Christ. I nevertheless feel obliged to state what commitments undergird my interpretive practice, in part because of the present-day conflict of hermeneutics and in part as a response to the apostolic exhortation: "Always be prepared to make a defense to

10. Ibid., 29.

any one who calls you to account for the hope that is in you" (1 Pet. 3:15).

Theory need not issue in a single methodological procedure. By "theory" I mean the articulation of the logic and the ideals that regulate interpretive practice and that distinguish legitimate from illegitimate interpretive practice. Theory describes the necessary features of good practice and explains *why* these features are characteristic of good practice. Theory articulates the regulative ideas (e.g., values, aims, norms) that our interpretive acts and practices always/already embody. It is through these articulations—and through dialogues such as we have represented in the present work—that our practices are confirmed, challenged, and corrected.

To paraphrase the Teacher: "Of the writing of hermeneutics there is no end." To be sure, the production of interpretation theories is hardly the primary aim of theological interpretation of Scripture. Where Kierkegaard could lament, "And then the interpretations—30,000 different interpretations,"[11] we may today feel more inclined to cry, "And then the hermeneutics!" Kierkegaard would doubtless be no more impressed by the proliferation of hermeneutical theories in our present day than he was by the proliferation of interpretations in his own. What he wanted was not a prolific but a primitive hermeneutics, a simple appropriation of the canonical discourse for one's own situation.

In the final analysis, neither interpreters nor hermeneutics should be prolific. The reader is not the begetter of meaning but rather a wet nurse who nurtures a discourse not of her own making. The text is a child of authorial discourse yet, precisely as begotten by authors, it can grow. As Gadamer says, "only the performance brings out everything that is in the play."[12] Elsewhere I have affirmed a "Pentecostal plurality" that maintains that the one true interpretation of a text is best approximated by a diversity of particular methods, contexts of reading, and interpretive communities.[13]

11. See Søren Kierkegaard, *For Self-Examination: Recommended for the Times* (trans. Edna Hong and Howard Hong; Minneapolis: Augsburg, 1940).

12. Hans-Georg Gadamer, *Truth and Method* (2nd rev. ed.; New York: Continuum, 2002), 147.

13. Vanhoozer, *Is There a Meaning in This Text?* 419.

If I have a theory concerning the one and the many in biblical interpretation, it amounts to what Mikhail Bakhtin calls creative understanding.[14] To understand creatively is progressively to discover the full, intrinsic meaning potential of authorial discourse through a process of reading texts in contexts other than the original. Reading Scripture with, for example, Lutherans, Methodists, and Episcopalians may bring to light certain aspects of the biblical text that one might not have seen by one's Presbyterian self.

Interpreters who discern previously unseen meaning potential in the text are not the begetters of this meaning but its witnesses. They recognize that the word of life that leads to the way of life has a life of its own that must be respected, protected, nurtured, and ministered. They practice not prolific but prolife hermeneutics. They know they are not the progenitors of this word and its meaning but its caretakers. Theological interpretation of Scripture is indeed a celebration of abundance, for it has as its focus the divine/human discourse that conveys the word of life, a word that continues to live, grow, and flourish wherever two or three are gathered to attend it.

14. See Mikhail Bakhtin, "Response to a Question from Novy Mir," in *Speech Genres and Other Late Essays* (Austin: University of Texas Press, 1986), 7.

8

Toward a Resolution
Yet to Be Revealed

···

A. K. M. ADAM

I was intrigued to read the other essays in this volume, as what
I read suggested both an increase in the degree to which our
positions converge and an increase in the nuance of our disagreements. That signals noteworthy progress toward a discourse in
which arguments actually contribute to clarity. The more clearly
we can frame our interpretive proposals, and the more carefully
we can distinguish them from alternatives, the more wisely we
can orient our work as expositors of Scripture—and, if necessary,
the more judiciously we can urge our colleagues to reconsider
their own orientation.

I welcome these signs of clarification, because I entered the
discussion of biblical theology at a moment when, it seemed,
a great aporia thwarted productive discussion of the issues involved. The way that historical-critical analysis dominated theo-

logical interpretation—not the *fact* that it dominated but the *way* that it dominated—effectively stifled imaginative inquiry into the relation of the Bible to theological thinking. Scholars, pastors, and students alike felt a common frustration when they tried to modulate from the excellent, rigorous exegetical work at which they had developed skill, to equally rigorous theological insight grounded in their technical analysis.

I felt a keen frustration at the ways that scholars proposed moving from analytical to expository interpretation. At the time, my studies with Brevard Childs provided the provocation that helped me stray from the broad road that modern biblical hermeneutics had paved, to explore byways and footpaths of interpretive practice.[1] I resolved to tackle two specific questions relative to biblical theology. First, I wondered how the theological tradition had managed for centuries to interpret Scripture in service of theological inquiry without the discomfort to which modern interpreters testified. Second, I wondered how to account for interpretive disagreement and how to account for readers' need to make interpretive judgments on matters where more-expert scholars had attained no consensus.

I tried to address the first topic by studying the transition from premodern perspectives on biblical theology to contemporary accounts (in the terminology that was then current, I compared "precritical" to "critical" biblical interpretation). On the basis of that work, I suggested that one source of interpretive problems derived from modern interpreters' tendency to elevate characteristics of their interpretive proclivities into transcendent norms for interpretation, when those proclivities owed as much (if not more) to identifiably cultural characteristics as they did to premises intrinsic to interpretation. The problem with modern biblical interpretation is not that it is modern, or wrong, but that many modern interpreters refuse to consider any other mode of interpretation legitimate.[2]

If modern interpretations might be sound enough on their own terms, but not exclusively valid, then we need all the more

1. Though I disagree with some particulars of Childs's approach to resolving interpretive challenges, I owe to his eloquent, winsome, encouraging instruction the critical perspective by which I argue on behalf of my different outlook.
2. A. K. M. Adam, *Making Sense of New Testament Theology* (Macon, GA: Mercer University Press, 1995).

urgently to learn how to think about interpretive difference. My study of postmodern theory suggested that conflicts over biblical interpretation might involve some considerations that the arguments themselves suppress. Critical scholars from a variety of fields show ways that the nature of verbal expression, historic conflicts, the effects of interpretive circumstances, and the importance of establishing incontrovertible arguments to support one's theological position (even when that constitutes claims that theology counts merely as an elaborated ideological fantasy)—in short: ambiguity, presuppositions, context, and power—affect our interpretations in ways that we cannot escape by more painstaking technical exegesis or by more obedient assent to what the church has always taught. In other words, since readers more pious, more erudite, and more intelligent than we are can arrive at divergent interpretations of a particular passage, we need a hermeneutic that clarifies interpretive differences even more than we need a hermeneutic that claims to lead us to correct answers.[3]

Since I have devoted particular effort to understanding interpretive difference, I appreciated the extent to which all three of the other essayists demonstrate a sensitive attention to aspects of this problem. Francis Watson's study of the ways that the early church rationalized the preeminence of four Gospels attends throughout to the critical imagination. The early church teachers devised ways of reconciling and interweaving the Gospels not simply because they found difference intolerable—otherwise they would have adopted Tatian's *Diatessaron*—but because the church understands difference to constitute an essential element of harmony.[4] Thus Watson shows us that the four-ness of the canonical Gospels cannot be said to derive its theological privi-

3. A. K. M. Adam, "The Sign of Jonah: A Fish-Eye View," *Semeia* 51 (1990): 177–91; idem, "Twisting to Destruction," *Perspectives on New Testament Ethics: Essays in Honor of Dan O. Via = Perspectives in Religious Studies* 23/2 (1996): 215–22; idem, "Walk This Way: Difference, Repetition, and the Imitation of Christ," *Interpretation* 55 (2001): 19–33; and idem, "Integral and Differential Hermeneutics," in *The Meanings We Choose: Hermeneutical Ethics, Indeterminacy and the Conflict of Interpretations* (ed. Charles H. Cosgrove; Journal for the Study of the Old Testament Supplement 411; Edinburgh: T&T Clark, 2004), 24–38.

4. Watson quotes Irenaeus's observation that the four Gospels are "consonant" with the four creatures of Revelation; the Greek word *symphōna* that Irenaeus uses already suggests the sphere of music as a fitting field of reference for iden-

lege from the four creatures of Elijah's heavenly chariot or from
the four creatures of Revelation; the variable explanations that
the early interpreters offer demonstrate that the interpretations
offer more-or-less plausible rationales for the number four, but
the explanations depend on the church having already arrived
at the sense that there should be four and only four Gospels.
As Watson points out, "there is no reason why five or six gospels should not have preserved the necessary coherence" with
scriptural tradition (see above, p. 107). Rather, the early church
made the imaginative discernment that, among the available accounts of Jesus and his teaching, *these four* preserved the truth
about Jesus in a breadth that afforded sufficient consonance to
ensure that they all pointed to the one Son, but with a fullness
that would have been impaired without the witness of all four. As
Watson shows, the appropriate, sound discernment that the four
canonical Gospels—and no others—should lend their authority
to the church's proclamation of Jesus's life and resurrection rests
not on the fathers' historical analysis of authorship and sources,
but on theological, ethical, and aesthetic criteria already shaped
by the tradition that the Gospels founded.

As the church takes up these canonical texts and ventures
to expound them, Kevin Vanhoozer offers a helpful character-
ization of theological interpretation of Scripture as a mode of
dramatic improvisation between the close of the canon and the
consummation foretold in Revelation. Interpreters may not simply disregard all that has gone before, wipe the historical slate
clean, and declare that now, at last, we have arrived at a sound
understanding of the scriptural script. In order to participate
responsibly and harmoniously in the shared performance of
this unscripted interval in church history, we must draw on the
extensive notes of our predecessors in the drama. Though we
do not exactly *reenact* their performances, we take up the cues
they offer us in order to shape our character in ways that cohere
with the biblical, church-historical precedents (on one hand)
and the eschatological conclusion (on the other).[5] In dramatic
improvisation, as in musical improvisation, "correctness" de-

---

tifying the theologically positive role of difference in interpretation. Ignatius
uses this metaphor as well, in his *To the Ephesians* 4.1–2; 5.1.

5. Here I thankfully deploy the useful terminology that Vanhoozer introduces
from Samuel Wells (*Improvisation: The Drama of Christian Ethics* [Grand Rapids:

rives from blending our voices and actions harmoniously and concordantly with the surrounding voices, rather than from identical reproduction or transposition of an authoritative paradigm. The discourse of improvisation allows the possibility that we may venture sound interpretation that would surprise our forebears without rupturing continuity with them; it offers a *bounded* freedom for interpretation. Perhaps in this model, biblical theologians function as drama coaches, who help inculcate certain sorts of interpretive habits, but who cannot dictate each improviser's specific performance.

Both the musical and the dramatic models reflect an approach to the theological interpretation of Scripture that draws much more heavily on a well-formed imagination than on the ephemeral certainty of an alleged scholarly consensus.[6] Such an approach requires of us vigilant attention to the question of how one identifies and inculcates a well-formed imagination—but then, it obviates the tendency to suppose that it is any easier to identify the uniquely correct exegetical basis for a theological interpretation. The experience of more than a hundred years of extraordinarily sophisticated historical-critical interpretation suggests that even a durable scholarly consensus may evanesce and that even a basic interpretive question may elicit multiple, plausible, technically sound answers. Under such circumstances, a reader who appeals to a unique plain sense or a determinate meaning often resorts to asserting academic unanimity in a voice loud enough to drown out dissent or to substituting a *favorite* interpretive theory for an *undoubtable* one.

The empirically verifiable diversity among avowedly literal interpretations thus tends to affirm the point that Stephen Fowl makes concerning Thomas Aquinas's hermeneutics. For Thomas as for us, the "literal sense" cannot be reduced to a single decisive, determinate meaning; as the unity of God and of the divine intention encounter us in multifarious ways, so we ought not "constrict the meaning of a text of Scripture in such a way as to preclude other truthful meanings." Fowl points out that Thomas's multifaceted literal sense makes it possible for Scrip-

---

Brazos, 2004]) and Keith Johnstone (*Impro: Improvisation and the Theatre* [New York: Routledge, 1981]).

6. Or, even less stable, on an individual scholar's claim to have arrived at a definitively correct interpretation of a biblical passage.

ture to inform our encounters with the inexhaustible variety of circumstances in human life; by the same token, though, the multifaceted literal sense integrates with our attempts to live out the gospel, attempts that will always stymie efforts to stave off ambiguity in the name of simple, unambiguous meaning. Fowl shows that the Parisian affinity for insisting that a "literal meaning" still always issues in interpretive plurality did not originate with twentieth-century poststructuralists, but reflects an inheritance from the fourteenth-century instruction of university lecturer Thomas Aquinas.

While the essays in this volume do not arrive at a concordant resolution—we are perhaps only in the thematic development of our theological *sonata allegro*—the distinct themes that resound in our essays seem to be reaching toward a resolution yet to be revealed. Frustrating though our present false notes and dissonances be, we eagerly await the eventual recapitulation that will bring our efforts into harmony with one another and the truth, when the friendship and mutual respect that provided the occasion for these essays is crowned with the perfectly shared insight to which the Bible points. In many and various ways, after all, God has spoken to us of old in the Scriptures, but someday we will understand fully, harmoniously, in the fifth act of the divine drama—though perhaps these four theologians will not cease in vivid discussion even then.

Index of Scripture
and Other Ancient Writings

Index of Subjects